Cambridge Elements ≡

Elements in Publishing and Book Culture
edited by
Samantha Rayner
University College London
Rebecca Lyons
University of Bristol

CHRISTMAS BOOKS FOR CHILDREN

Eugene Giddens
Anglia Ruskin University

CAMBRIDGE
UNIVERSITY PRESS

CAMBRIDGE
UNIVERSITY PRESS

University Printing House, Cambridge CB2 8BS, United Kingdom

One Liberty Plaza, 20th Floor, New York, NY 10006, USA

477 Williamstown Road, Port Melbourne, VIC 3207, Australia

314–321, 3rd Floor, Plot 3, Splendor Forum, Jasola District Centre,
New Delhi – 110025, India

79 Anson Road, #06–04/06, Singapore 079906

Cambridge University Press is part of the University of Cambridge.

It furthers the University's mission by disseminating knowledge in the pursuit of
education, learning, and research at the highest international levels of excellence.

www.cambridge.org
Information on this title: www.cambridge.org/9781108741385
DOI: 10.1017/9781108590259

A catalogue record for this publication is available from the British Library.

First published 2019

ISBN 978-1-108-74138-5 Paperback
ISSN 2514-8524 (online)
ISSN 2514-8516 (print)

Christmas Books for Children

Elements in Publishing and Book Culture

DOI: 10.1017/9781108590259

First published online: November 2019

Eugene Giddens

Anglia Ruskin University

Author for correspondence: Eugene Giddens, eugene.giddens@anglia.ac.uk

ABSTRACT: This Element traces the varied and magical history of Christmas publications for children. The Christmas book market has played an important role in the growth of children's literature, from well-loved classics to more ephemeral annuals and gift books. Starting with the eighteenth century and continuing to recent sales successes and picturebooks, Christmas Books for Children investigates continuities and new trends in this hugely significant part of the children's book market.

KEYWORDS: Children's literature, Christmas, publishing, Dickens, Santa Claus

ISBNs: 9781108741385 (PB), 9781108590259 (OC)

ISSNs: 2514-8524 (online), 2514-8516 (print)

Contents

Introduction

Where Christmas books begin publishers know best; where they end nobody will ever know. What are, and what are not, Christmas books? Who shall say? Is everything which sees the light for the last six weeks of the year a Christmas book?

'Christmas Books', *The Saturday Review*, 30 November 1867, 707

The Christmas market played a large part in the emergence of the 'golden age' of children's literature. Books became idealised as the perfect Christmas gifts for young people; that publishing culture in turn became responsible for the phenomenal sales successes of, for instance, the picture-books of Walter Crane and Kate Greenaway and the longer-form prose of Charles Dickens and Lewis Carroll. An expectation of high pre-Christmas sales made it possible to specialise, as an author, illustrator, or publisher, in children's books.

Since the invention of Christmas gifts in the 1820s, books have been seen as the most appropriate offerings for children. In 1821, the very first historical mention of Santa Claus bringing presents, for instance, places books above toys:

> Old Santeclaus with much delight
> His reindeer drives this frosty night,
> O'er chimneytops, and tracks of snow,
> To bring his yearly gifts to you ...
> No drums to stun their Mother's ear,
> Nor swords to make their sisters fear;
> But pretty books to store their mind
> With knowledge of each various kind.
>
> *Children's Friend*, 1821, np

Equally, children's books can be said to have facilitated, if not driven, the wider cultural growth of Christmas from the Victorian period onwards. The fashions of Christmas are continually renegotiated in children's books in the nineteenth century, from the rise of newfangled Christmas trees to the loss of traditions such as wassailing and the boar's head. Christmas is not merely an agreed set of static family experiences, but changes dynamically because of the influence of print media, including books, periodicals, and, from 1843, Christmas cards. Christmas matures more slowly in the twentieth century, to be sure, but that change is also inspired by books and adaptations of them in other media, especially TV and film. Contemporary trends such as Carol V. Aebersold and Chanda A. Bell's *The Elf on the Shelf* (Atlanta, GA, 2005) continue to emerge out of popular works of seasonal fiction. Today 'Super Thursday' in October witnesses the launch of major children's (and adult) books for the Christmas sales period, making it one of the most important events in the publishing calendar. When children's books miss that first Thursday of the month, they often come out soon thereafter, like Philip Pullman's *La Belle Sauvage* of 19 October 2017 or the runaway bestseller of Christmas 2017 in the United Kingdom, David Walliams' *Bad Dad*, 2 November 2017. This trend of concentrating sales over a brief holiday season in fact emerged in the early nineteenth century in Britain and America.[1] By tracing the history of Christmas publishing, this short monograph examines festive books as part of children's publishing's most important season.

In order to understand the full context of children's Christmas books, I consider the earliest holiday works for children and compare that original context to contemporary trends. I primarily focus on the early Christmas market, up to 1910, as authors and publishers at that time developed a set of marketing and dissemination practices that have remained largely static: because they work. The final section examines how those publishing conventions have been retained and renegotiated in more recent books (mostly 2000–2018, but touching upon seminal developments in the twentieth century). In some respects, 'Christmas books' can define most literature for children, as books from *Alice's Adventures in Wonderland* to the final Harry Potter volumes

---

[1] If not earlier, as M. O. Grenby points out of the famous eighteenth-century children's publisher John Newbery: 'Francis Newbery suggested that the Christmas market dominated children's publishing, hyperbolically recalling that "an edition of many thousands" of his father's books could be "sometimes exhausted during the Christmas holidays"' (*Child Reader*, 2011, 172).

have had releases timed to take advantage of gift sales. Because one-third of books sold in a given year might be bought over the Christmas period, I have limited my corpus to titles that are explicitly marketed as seasonal books, usually with keywords in the title like 'present', 'gift', 'Santa', or, of course, 'Christmas'. For the most part these books signal their festive subject matter through titles, but sometimes other paratexts such as blurbs, chapter titles, or frontispieces are used to that effect. Some books, like Karina Yan Glaser's *The Vanderbeekers of 141st Street* (2017), are subtle about their Christmas subject matter; the inner dust jacket flap discloses that 'It's five days before Christmas . . . What the Vanderbeekers need now is a Christmas miracle.' Digital marketing of the book by publisher (hmhbooks.com) and author (karinaglaser.com) makes this setting more apparent. Other works do not mention Christmas in the paratexts, but do so early in the narrative, as with *Little Women* (1868), where it is famously the first word. Such subtlety is a reminder that most of the books sold for children over the Christmas holidays are not actually about Christmas. Amazon's children's bestsellers on 19 December 2017 at 7 p.m., for instance, had no Christmas titles for the US list and only one, Tom Fletcher's *The Christmasaurus*, on the UK list (at number four). Clearly, the books that are actually given to children over Christmas year by year become far too large a corpus for critical consideration – it could include almost any title – so I do not attempt to engage with that wider sense of market here.

This Element reflects the study of nearly 400 Christmas or holiday books from Mary Collyer's *A Christmass-Box* of 1746 to Michael Morpurgo's *Grandpa Christmas* of 2018. I have been lucky to consult much of the early and some of the later material at the Baldwin Library, University of Florida. Almost all of the books examined here come from either the nineteenth or the twenty-first century. I realise that this selection neglects long-standing favourites, such as John Masefield's *Box of Delights* (1935), Alison Uttley's *Little Grey Rabbit's Christmas* (1939), Raymond Briggs' *The Snowman* (1978), and even Dr Seuss' *How the Grinch Stole Christmas!* (1957). Such books will be alluded to in passing, and my temporal bias is borne out of a sense that many printed classics from the twentieth century derive their publishing frameworks and Christmassy topics from earlier periods. The 'Christmas Box' is the eighteenth-century precursor to the box of delights, for instance, while the Grinch humorously redeploys the Scrooge tradition. Equally, the twentieth-century market could be considered large enough to constitute an additional book by itself. By bookending the broad history of such works, I aim to give a sense of origins, innovations, and continuities.

My selection of books also reveals a geographical bias, borne in part out of my concentration on books in English. Almost all American and British Christmas books from the nineteenth century are published in Boston, New York, Philadelphia, London, or, more rarely, Edinburgh, sometimes in multiple editions across these cities. It is difficult to get a sense of a US Southern family's Christmas – in part because publishing was centred in the north-east, and even more so of a Christmas in Australia or as lived by Californian Chinese immigrants (although these experiences exist as kinds of othering 'foils' in many children's Christmas texts).[2] Early Christmas books represent the holiday as an amalgam of New England townhouse, London hovel, or English country house – a strange mixture that persists in shaping Christmas throughout the nineteenth century, as I show in what follows. More variety, including texts written in dual languages, is found in my analysis of twenty-first-century books, but by and large the Christmas market continues to be dominated by the major publishing houses operating out of New York and London, and inevitably this Element partially replicates US and UK biases. Most of the books discussed in the final section are chosen because they top bestseller lists (e.g. Amazon's dynamic lists and those published in *The Bookseller*) in the twenty-first century, or because they offer pioneering inflections to the genre.

Any work on *Christmas children's books* must engage with those key terms, across various times and places. Instead of focusing only on 'Christmas', I deliberately include books on Hanukkah, Kwanzaa, and the New Year, participating as they do not only as significant religious and cultural holidays, but also in children's seasonal book culture, particularly that of the twenty-first century. Books such as Virginia Hamilton's *Bluish* (New York, 1999) tackle wider diversity issues through children's under-standings of different approaches to the holidays. Inclusivity here is part

---

[2] For historical, mostly adult, perspectives from the enslaved and the enslavers, see 'Christmas in the Slave South' (Restad, *Christmas in America*, 1995, 75–90).

of how holiday narratives can work. My corpus represents a variety of points on a scale from devoutly religious to entirely secular, but it must be said that nineteenth-century texts placing heavy emphasis on Jesus as 'the reason for the season' tend to show some disdain for Christmas gifts as I show in Section 2 – and therefore Christmas books, except for the Bible. I also adopt a permissive definition of what constitutes a book for *children*. Often the works under consideration here are directly marketed towards young readers or listeners, but I have been attentive to the flexible approach advocated by Marah Gubar's 'On Not Defining Children's Literature' (2011). Sometimes it is difficult to pinpoint what makes a children's book – *A Visit from St Nicholas* is a prime example of an adult text that becomes a children's poem only over time. A final word about *books*: I have concentrated here on the physical codex, not its relatives in magazines, games, apps, e-readers, and other electronic media. Children's magazines are popular over the Christmas period, of course, but their year-round publication, typically monthly, precludes them from being considered seasonal books. Digital children's books, at least in terms of sales, continue to do surprisingly poorly, as publishers' figures have shown for several years.[3] My attention to publishing history focuses on works in print as a better way of tracing continuities and departures over time across a single format.

Christmas books are a dauntingly broad category, for which I can hope only to provide a snapshot. A consideration of the beginnings of the genre and most recent developments helps to point to a trajectory without covering each divergent path and novelty along the way. Nonetheless, I aim to demonstrate that children's Christmas books, while not wavering in significance to the publishing industry in the past 200 years, have actively reshaped cultural understandings of the holiday season – being producers as much as mirrors of it.

---

[3] 'The steepest decline in e-book sales last year was in the children's category, where sales fell 22%', Jim Milliot, 'E-book Sales Fell 10% in 2017', *Publishers Weekly*, 25 April 2018. www.publishersweekly.com/pw/by-topic/digital/con tent-and-e-books/article/76706-e-book-sales-fell-10-in-2017.html

1 The Emergence and Growth of the Christmas Book Market, 1750–1850

The Earliest Children's Christmas Books

Before there are Christmas stockings or trees, or even Christmas gifts, there are Christmas texts. Ben Jonson's *Christmas His Masque* (London, 1641), written as a royal entertainment for 1616, includes the characters of Carol, Misrule, Wassail, and New-Year's-Gift, as well as Minced-Pie and even Cupid. Father Christmas here takes the traditional English role of presiding over very adult festivities. Robert Herrick specialises in poems for the season in the 1640s, mixing topics ranging from sacred hymns to bawdy customs, including 'drink[ing] to your hearts' desiring' (*Hesperides*, 1898, 79). These seventeenth-century texts, like the Christmases they represent, are largely adult-focused, revealing communities sharing food, copious drink, and the occasional merry prank or show. Puritanical discomfort with Christmas of course points its animosity to such excesses. But whether in favour of Christmas festivities or against them, this large part of the history of the holiday has little to do with giving to children. Children's Christmas books come significantly later, and can be found to date from the very beginning of children's literature itself. M. O. Grenby has shown that 'the marketing of children's books as gifts began early. Mary Collyer's *A Christmas-Box for Masters and Misses* was published by M. Cooper and M. Boreman in 1746. By 1750 John Newbery had followed suit with *Nurse Truelove's Christmas-Box* and *Nurse Truelove's New-Year's Gift*' (Grenby, *Child Reader*, 2011, 170). As Andrea Immel notes of *Christmass-Box*: 'Although the title is most attractive, its contents disappoint by failing to reveal anything about Georgian holiday traditions' ('*A Christmass-Box*', 2009, 1). *Nurse Truelove* similarly compiles secular, moral stories that are not about the season. Children's Christmas books in this early phase, therefore, have little to do with Christmas. One of the earliest Christmas children's books is in fact a gift *from* young people: *A Christmas Offering, Humbly Presented by the Charity Children, of Christ Church* (London, 1788), contains a single song, printed to raise money for the poor.

These first Christmas books are part of a gift-book tradition that attempts to tap into any cause for celebration, whether birthday, Christmas, or New Year. A series of books called *A Present for Children* (Edinburgh from 1761) contains 'catechisms ... moral songs ... prayers and graces', but make no reference to the Christmas season. Similarly Dorothy Kilner's *The Holyday Present* (London, 1781) represents children being naughty or nice in a distinctly summer setting; J. D. Parry's *The Anthology: An Annual Reward Book for Midsummer and Christmas* (London, 1830) makes its suitability for either summer or winter apparent in the title. Elizabeth Somerville's *A Birth Day Present; or A New Year's Gift. Being Nine Day's Conversation between a Mother and Daughter, on Interesting Subjects; for the Use of Young Persons, from Ten to Fifteen Years of Age* (Boston, 1803; printed earlier in London) also cannot make up its mind as to occasion, although an editor's note shows that the book was published in time for the Christmas season by wishing readers '*A HAPPY NEW YEAR*' (np). There had long been a tradition of giving New Year's gifts, as the character of that name in Jonson's masque implies, and the full shift to Christmas giving occurs only in the early nineteenth century. Many books retain their leaning towards 'New Year' as the appropriate holiday for gifts until the 1820s. *Original Tales; Never before Published. Designed as a New-Year's Gift for the Youth of Both Sexes* (Boston, 1813) promises in its advertisement to 'blend amusement with instruction' (np). *A New-Year's Gift* (New York, 1809) is an alphabet book with each page hosting a miniature woodcut and two Bible verses, being the earliest instance I can find of a holiday alphabet. A. Selwyn's *A New Year's Gift; or, Domestic Tales for Children* (London, 1824) is a very pretty example, with marbled boards as binding, but it too selects moral tales that make no mention of Christmas or New Year.[4] Books here represent an opportunity to occupy children within the household, making Christmas a chance for independent study as much as a family celebration. These early gift books tend towards heavy moralising, or they provide games, riddles, and

---

[4] The copy held by the Baldwin Library, University of Florida, has a gift inscription, 'Amelia Britten Jan^{ry} – 1st – 1830 from her brother JB', suggesting that it was an actual New Year's gift.

'pastimes' to occupy a class of child reader who is clearly home from school. All of them eschew representations of actual Christmas festivities, partially, I suspect, because such celebrations were highly varied – ranging from a semi-Puritanical avoidance of the holiday altogether, to religious celebration, to more secular, 'pagan' even, excesses of dancing and ale. Today it would be inconceivable for a children's Christmas book not even to mention the season, but in the eighteenth century it was the norm.

By the turn of the century Christmas begins to make its way into holiday books. Anna Laetitia Barbauld and John Aikin's *New Christmas Tales, Forming the Second Part of Evenings at Home* (London, *c.*1790) makes the class and educational aspirations apparent from the very beginning. The setting is: 'The mansion-house of the pleasant village of Beachgrove ... inhabited by the family of Fairborne, consisting of the master and mistress, and a numerous progeny of children of both sexes' (1). The educational activity (and narrative framework) of the tales comes in the form of a story box, to which every child is expected to contribute: 'As some of them were accustomed to writing, they would frequently produce a fable, a story, or dialogue, adapted to the age and understanding of the young people' (1). These stories are placed in a locked box and randomly selected; they include morals, natural history, travelogues, engineering, and science. The country house location recalls an old-fashioned Christmas for the community, but here it becomes concentrated to family members, especially children, omitting the social strata of local tradespeople who would in former decades have expected to partake in the squire's bounty. The how-to-behave books for stately Christmases occupy a minor subgenre throughout the nineteenth century, most famously in Washington Irving's book of *Old Christmas* (first published 1819). Other early examples include the self-explanatory *Christmas Holidays, or The Young Visitants; a Tale; in Which Many Pleasant Descriptions of That Festive Season, Both in Town and Country, Are Given for the Benefit of the Rising Generation* (London, 1806) and Sarah Wheatly's *The Christmas Fire-Side; or, The Juvenile Critics* (London, 1806). *Christmas Holidays* demonstrates a great deal of class-based particularity, with one father willing to welcome his son's friend only when he learns his lineage: 'a gentleman of independent property, that one of his family had been high sheriff of the county, and that [his mother] was a baronet's daughter' (8). Interestingly the book keeps some of the old festive master-servant relations that are more slowly released in Britain than the United States. The young boys venture

> into the servant's hall, where many of the good people of the village had been invited with their families to partake of a Christmas dinner; and where, while the nut-brown ale was cheerfully passing round, a band of morrice [*sic*] dancers were displaying their agility, while the low humour and buffoonery of their clown, drew peals of laughter and applause from the merry hearted company. (15–16)

Their country holiday includes shooting and singing. When they reverse the exchange into the city they find a much more sombre table:

> Not a word of conversation passed during the time of dinner, except what was merely necessary for helping each other to eatables; as Mr. Pierpoint would have deemed it an unpardonable offence, had any pleasantry, which might have escaped him or any of his family, excited a smile on the features of any of his attendants. (37)

They do, however, get to attend the theatre. Wheatley uses a round-robin storytelling framework, like Barbauld and Aiken, and, like them too, she carefully vouches for the quality of the family who retell the stories: 'At Holly Hall, in the county of Devon, the family of Arborfield had resided for several centuries; and had always been remarkable for maintaining the true English character of integrity, benevolence, and hospitality' (1). Propriety is retained at all costs in these earliest representations of Christmas holidays.

Many of the stories from this period are not what we would today regard as child-friendly, some deliberately so. Solomon Sobersides, the moral pseudonym for the author of *Christmas Tales for the Amusement and Instruction of Young Ladies and Gentlemen in Winter Evenings* (New York, 1794), offers an instructive framework on the title page: 'The cheerful Sage, when solemn dictates fail, / Conceals the moral Counsel in – a Tale.'[5] He continues by admonishing parents and teachers in the Preface: 'There is nothing, in reality, where people are so very wrong as in the education of children' (5). Sobersides' attempts at education are highly adult-centric. The first story, for instance, is about a wicked daughter-in-law who convinces a son 'under the sole dominion of his wife' to be cruel to his father (7). The final story features an execution, complete with a woodcut of a man hanging from the gallows, with the moral: 'so he fell a sacrifice to his own folly, and died unpitied, because unknown' (125). Christmas and death have a powerful connection in this period, one that continues for the next 100 years.

A greater sense that children need to be entertained, as well as warned, as part of their instruction emerges from the turn of the century. *Mince Pies for Christmas, and for All Merry Seasons* (London, 1807; 1805), for instance, notes in the Preface that children are becoming tired of pure pedagogy in the holidays: '"What a trick!" will mammy's pampered darling exclaim, "I was expected to have found something that was pleasant to my palate, and not a mess of things to puzzle my brains"' (v). As if to show that the rebuses in the pages to follow will not suit everyone, the frontispiece has three ebullient children alongside one who appears to have a headache.

Mince Pies, despite its didactic nature, is one of the few early Christmas books to be aimed at child readers, as opposed to repackaging stories for adults:

> [T]he good boys and girls of this kingdom … value an
> intellectual treat, as much as you do solid pies and pastry;
> and … while they are spending their Christmas holidays at
> home, would find some hours lie heavy on their hands, if
> they had not a new book to take up, when other festivities
> grew insipid. (vi)

Occasionally the riddles are a little ribald – ' … a virgin, a bawd, and a Franciscan friar … ' (93) – but generally the puzzles connect to class-room themes: 'A word of three syllables, seek 'till you find, / That has in

---

[5] This work is printed earlier in Edinburgh, and later in Worcester, Massachusetts, as *A Pretty New Year's Gift*.

See here the Youth by Wisdom led,
The paths of life securely tread;
The dang'rous lures of Folly shun,
And Virtue's course serenely run.

CHRISTMAS TALES,

FOR THE

Amusement and Instruction

OF

Young Ladies & Gentlemen

IN

WINTER EVENINGS.

By SOLOMON SOBERSIDES.

The chearful Sage, when solemn dic-
tates fail,
Conceals the moral Counsel in---a
Tale.

Printed in Hudson (*New-York*) by
ASHBEL STODDARD, and sold
at his Book Store, Wholesale and
Retail. M,DCC,XCIV.

Figure 1 Solomon Sobersides, *Christmas Tales* (New York, 1794), frontispiece and title page – Baldwin Library, University of Florida – 15h8083

it the twenty-four letters combin'd' (4). A decade later, there is more such scope for play. E. Sandham's *The Grandfather, or The Christmas Holidays* (London, 1816) has shifted almost entirely in aims towards seeking 'a kind reception from all her young readers' by offering the book 'not as a task to be performed, but as an agreeable instructive amusement' (np).

As these earliest examples show, several publishers had been keen to build their children's Christmas book market across the late 1700s and early 1800s. Booksellers and shops soon followed. Stephen Nissenbaum has combed newspaper advertisements in search of the early marketing of gifts for children: 'The very first advertisement I have found for Christmas presents, the 1806 one from Salem, Massachusetts, was for "a

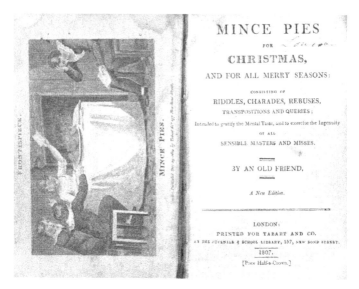

Figure 2 *Mince Pies for Christmas, and for All Merry Seasons* (London, 1807), title page and frontispiece – Baldwin Library, University of Florida – 15h98

large assortment of Youth's and Children's Books." The first ad from Boston, in 1808, was for "Books for Children"' (*Battle for Christmas*, 1996, 136). Nissenbaum's findings demonstrate the centrality of the children's book to the emerging Christmas gift market. Many of these books would not have been Christmas-specific. Bibles, Psalms, and other books intended for adult readers dominate the gift market throughout the early-to-mid nineteenth century. It is little surprise that the girls in Louisa May Alcott's *Little Women* (1868) receive Bibles in various bindings. Nonetheless, hints at a new type of Christmas children's literature, with an emphasis on 'amusement' over the holidays, begin to emerge.

The 1820s–1830s

The British Library holds eighty-eight items with 'Christmas' in the title and dated to 1750–1800. The vast majority of these are religious materials –

sermons, hymns, etc. – for adults, with only two explicitly directed to children. From 1801 to 1820, however, seventy items emerge, including eleven titles that invoke a youthful subject matter or readership, with words such as 'child', 'juvenile', 'young', 'boys', and 'girls'. As Stephen Nissenbaum has shown, the holiday underwent a shift to child-centeredness around 1820. The prosperous, instead of upholding the semi-feudal tradition of giving gifts to servants and tradespeople, switched rapidly towards a culture of providing presents for their children or for the children of their extended families (Nissenbaum, *Battle for Christmas*, 1996, 62). With the movement to child-centeredness comes a greater desire to please – in addition to instruct – the child recipient.

The 1820s also saw such innovations as the invention of Santa Claus as we know him today and a culture of stocking-filling, moving away from the gift boxes that had their origins in tradespeople's collection boxes. Henry Livingston's *A Visit from St Nicholas*, first published in 1823 and usually ascribed to Clement Clarke Moore, makes the most famous contribution towards these shifts, although it is not until two decades later that the poem is published for children.[6] Nissenbaum has also shown that the first appearance of Saint Nicholas as a bearer of Christmas gifts comes in the 1821 publication *The Children's Friend* (*Battle for Christmas*, 1996, 73), not in *A Visit from St Nicholas*. *The Children's Friend* includes an illustration of Santa on a sleigh with one reindeer. The sleigh is labelled 'REWARDS' and contains dolls and books. Tellingly, the poem is very specific about what constitutes appropriate toys:

> To some I gave a pretty doll,
> To some a peg-top, or a ball;
> No crackers, cannons, squibs, or rockets,
> To blow their eyes up, or their pockets . . .
> I left an apple, or a tart,
> Or wooden gun, or painted cart. (3–5)

---

[6] The poem originally appears in a local paper out of Troy, New York, the *Sentinel*, so ostensibly it targets adult readers. On the poem's authorship, and the probability that it was written by Livingston, see Jackson, *Who Wrote 'The Night Before Christmas'?*, 2016.

An appropriate rule even for today, noise-makers are excluded in favour of toys, although the book has an illustration of a boy being blinded by fireworks that seems excessively punitive. *The Children's Friend* closes with a warning that poorly behaved children will receive a 'birchen rod' (8), beginning the idea of Santa having lists of naughty and nice boys and girls.

Although Livingston's famous *A Visit from St Nicholas* might not have been the first story about Santa, it certainly popularised the idea of a sleigh and reindeer, a sack full of toys, and a nimble way with chimneys. The first version of the poem published as an independent volume appears around 1848. Spalding and Shepard's 1849 publication is illustrated with black-and-white woodcuts and is 'A Present for Good Little Boys and Girls' (Livingston, *A Visit from St Nicholas*, np), if a small one at 12 cm by 16 cm. Thomas Nast illustrated the book in a picturebook format for Aunt Louisa's Big Picture Series (McLoughlin, *c.*1872); David Scattergood illustrated it for Degan, Estes and Company around 1880. Today the poem is probably the most heavily illustrated, in terms of the number of artists who have reimagined it, in all of children's literature. Scattergood's illustration for 'A Visit from Santa-Claus' (Figure 3) adds a tree, an innovation not in the original poem, as Christmas trees did not commonly exist in the United States in the 1820s.

The publication history of 'A Visit from Santa-Claus' could occupy its own tome – the Baldwin Library alone has twenty-six copies for children – but it was not immediately popular as a children's book. In many ways it is ahead of its time, but the nod and wink it gives to parents, encouraging them to fill their children's stockings, is probably more significant in changing cultures of Christmas than any other holiday book. Yet it also has a conservative force – owing entirely to its popularity – in ossifying a nostalgic vision that continues to shape present-day experience.

To get a sense of children's Christmas books in the 1820s and 1830s, however, one must look elsewhere. The residual publishing culture of moral tales – not mere fun celebrations with a naughty saint – holds firm. Edmund Butcher's *The New Year's Gift; or, Moral Tales Designed to Instruct and Improve the Minds of Youth* (Boston, 1819; first printed in London) is representative of this genre, with the title very much true to the contents.

A VISIT FROM

SANTA CLAUS.

BY

CLEMENT C. MOORE.

WAS the night before Christmas, when all
thro' the house
Not a creature was stirring, not even a mouse;

The stockings were hung by the chimneys with care,
In hopes that St. Nicholas soon would be there;

3

Figure 3 David Scattergood's illustration in 'A Visit from Santa-Claus'
(Boston, *c.*1880), p. 3 – Baldwin Library, University of Florida – 39p1478

One story, subtitled 'Female Excellence the Source of Real Felicity', tells of capitalist Charles inducted to religion by his new wife, Lucinda. The copy in the Baldwin Library is peppered with family names, suggesting passage through the generations as a work of lasting value, but like other early nineteenth-century gift books, it has simple marbled-paper boards and a small 10 cm by 14 cm format that does not speak to any great cost. It also has an initial gift inscription from 16 January 1820, pointing out how the holiday or New Year season might be broadly conceived.

So far, with the exception of the *New-Year's Gift* of 1809 mentioned previously, very few early Christmas books are published for very young or pre-readers. Mary Hughs' *Aunt Mary's New Year's Gift to Good Little Boys and Girls Who Are Learning to Read* (London, 1819) aims to exploit that gap in the market with four short stories, including one very much on topic, 'The Little Girl Who Did Not Like to Learn to Read'. Again, the book is cheaply produced and small, 10 cm by 13 cm, with marbled-paper boards. A. Selwyn's *A New Year's Gift; or, Domestic Tales for Children* (London, 1824) adopts the same format, revealing a mini-vogue for small, slight gift books in paper bindings. The Baldwin Library copy of Hughs' text is inscribed from one sister to another, and its copy of Selwyn's book is inscribed from a brother to a sister, showing how children might provide such economical books as gifts themselves. Not only parents, aunts, or uncles bought them.

By the end of the 1820s, Christmas books take a darker tone, and the moralising, despite the invention of jolly Santa, becomes paradoxically heavier and less accommodating. *The Literary Box: Containing the Contributions of the Evelyn Family* (Philadelphia, PA, [1826]) has children warning their own parents that 'however indulgent you may be, you [should] always tell us of our faults' (40) and a grandpa who threatens to keep a recalcitrant child 'upon bread and water for a week; this would soon have brought him round' (94). Such punishment narratives might seem strong enough, but this decade delights also in illness and death stories, a surprisingly common trope in children's Christmas books. Harriet Martineau's protagonist, Sarah, watches her father die in *Christmas Day; or, The Friends* (London, 1825) and learns 'not to look forward with too much confidence of enjoyment to another year' (39). Sarah suffers another terrible Christmas fate in Martineau's follow-up, *The Friends:*

A Continuation of 'Christmas-Day' (London, 1826): 'When the holidays came, Sarah . . . obtained the opinion of an eminent physician about the state of her sight. . . . She was now certain that total blindness was to be her lot' (65). Eliza Leslie's *The Gift* (1838) does not live up to the cheerful promise of its title, with stories instead of the 'Request of the Dying Child' and 'The Capuchin's Death'. *The Warning Clock, or, The Voice of the New Year* (New York, 1829) offers an allegory of two sisters, Diligence and Indolence. The title page itself warns against affection for holiday books, almost punishing the recipient of the book for even being appreciative of it:

> While this gay toy attracts thy sight,
> Thy reason let it warn;
> And seize, my dear, the rapid time,
> That never shall return!

Ultimately Indolence is cast into Hell: 'to the dark and dreadful abode of the slothful and unprofitable servant, to the above of *outer darkness, where there is weeping, and wailing, and gnashing of teeth: where the worm dieth not, and the fire is not quenched*' (16). The book deals in a kind of holiday trick, reminding young readers of their impending doom in order to spark a 'Christian' work ethic.

These more foreboding texts point to a backlash against the new, secular, and child-focused version of Christmas festivities competing at around the same time. Texts taking a more obviously Christian perspective on Christmas struggled to accommodate the increasingly materialistic culture of giving. *Julia Changed; or, The True Secret of a Happy Christmas*, published by the American Sunday School Union in 1831, seems concerned to offer a revisionist approach to the season. The heroine, Julia, breaks her arm at the beginning of the narrative and agrees to spend her recuperation time reading to younger children. She determines, after reading the nativity story in Luke, to ask for no presents at all and indeed wishes to die, saying to Jesus: 'oh, take me now, – take my body and my soul to-day – thy birth-day' (55–6). The refusing or regifting of presents would become a dominant motif in later Christmas books for children.

Rejections of the new Christmas also come in the form of nostalgia, or for American readers as a yearning for English models (generally, if surprisingly, as opposed to Dutch or German ones). *A Fireside Book, or The Account of a Christmas Spent at Old Court* (London, 1830; second edition) represents 'Christmas at Old Court 1712', where 'the guests first considered were the poor and needy' and 'barrels of good strong ale were kept flowing' (26). The ubiquity of the English experience is reflected in *Peter Parley's Tales about Christmas* (1838/9), which has an international audience reflected by printings in London, New York, Dublin, Glasgow, Sydney, and Hobart Town. The preface to the New York edition asserts that 'whatever Christmas customs we have, are derived from England' (viii). Parley's Christmas harks back to a time before child-centric celebrations:

> If you were to ask me what English people mean when they speak of Christmas, it would puzzle me to tell you, for it seems to me that Christmas is, in their minds, made up of religious feeling, of acts of charity, holiday, and fireside enjoyment; of church-going, alms-giving, and family-gathering. Christmas carols, and pleasant acquaintance, crackling faggots, and farm-house fare; bunches of holly, and boughs of mistletoe; smoking joints, and foaming beer; laughing, story-telling, and blind-man's-buff, are all contained in the word Christmas. (5)

He also describes 'the bristly boar' (275–6), whose head crowned the feast, and goes into great detail about the 'custom of ornamenting our houses and churches with evergreens' (284). Lest this should seem too secular for any Puritanical colonists, Parley assures his readers that church and celebration are kept in balance: 'The honest farmer . . . was equally particular in setting an example in church-going and convivial mirth' (321). The implication here is that the 'new' secular Christmas is not very novel at all, but the balance has tilted too far away from community. Other books are concerned with teaching children the practicalities of a traditional Christmas. Lydia Maria Child's *Girl's Own Book* (London and Glasgow, 1832) offers, for instance, detailed instructions on how 'To Preserve Roses Till Christmas' (249). It should be noted, too, that publishers continued to take advantage of the Christmas market by publishing collections of 'Christmas Tales' that had nothing to do with the season. *Christmas Stories, Containing John Wildgoose, the Poacher; The Smuggler; and Good-Nature, or, Parish Matters* (London, 1835; fourth edition) instead warns children of the dangers of trafficking illegal goods. T. Crofton Croker's collection, *The Christmas Box, an Annual Present for Children* (London, 1828), has only one seasonal item, a single-page poem called 'A Christmas Carol' with lines including 'Patés – Patés – Patés – Patés' and 'Pudding – pudding – pudding – pudding' in celebration of the festive table (188).

Already by the 1830s there are competing modes of Christmas in children's books. Although Santa is reinvented, he by no means becomes common. Gift-giving to children is normalised, however, and despite some backlash against holiday mercantilism, there is a healthy market for children's books, including cheap and short books that clearly take advantage of the opportunity to supply a burgeoning market for seasonal presents.

The Familiar Christmas: Trees, Stockings, and Santa

Christmas becomes Christmas as we know it from the 1840s. The Baldwin Library contains thirty-three books with 'Christmas' in the title in this decade, compared to the twenty-two of the 1830s. Such 1840s festive books contribute disproportionately to form a modern Christmas. Mrs Percy Sinnett is conscious of this cultural moment, noting in her book: 'These customs are ... amazingly in favour with the children, [so] there is what is called a powerful interest enlisted in their preservation ... it may probably be very long before they die away altogether' (*Story about a Christmas*, 1846, 2). Children's books such as Sinnett's, ostensibly tasked with 'preservation', in fact help to create these traditions. Christmas trees, stockings, and Santa begin by 1840 to become the dominant tropes that they remain today in seasonal books for children. Meanwhile, while books continue to be seen as the ideal presents, a self-sustaining cycle emerges whereby gift books advocate the purchase of other gift books.

Santa and stockings fill the anonymous *Saint Nicholas's Book for All Good Boys and Girls* (Philadelphia, PA, 1842). The title page has two fireplace stocking scenes and two Santas, one at the top and one at the bottom of a chimney (Figure 4). It here becomes essential that children hang up stockings for Santa; Christmas boxes are long gone:

> He brings with him a good number of toys, pretty books,
> bon bons, and other presents such as all young folks delight
> in, and having descended the chimney, he deposits
> a quantity in the stocking of each of the good children,
> providing always, that they have duly hung their stocking
> up in the chimney corner before going to bed.
>
> *Saint Nicholas's Book*, 1842, 5

As a validation of this position, *Saint Nicholas's Book* reprints *A Visit from St Nicholas* as its first piece. It also carefully asserts that books, particularly this book, make the best presents: 'Each of those children whom Saint Nicholas, or Kriss Kringle most highly approves, will be sure to find a copy of this book, with all its stories and pictures, and its nice binding, safely deposited in his stocking . . . on the morning of Christmas, or at farthest, next New Year's Day' (6). Pity the brothers or sisters who received a different book.

With Santa and stockings firmly entrenched, the new festive part of the season is the Christmas tree. Although Christmas trees had been erected and decorated in central Europe since the early modern period, and come to Britain from Germany at the beginning of the nineteenth century through the marriage ties of the royal family, they are popular in American children's literature from the 1840s. These early books are careful to emphasise the German origins of the ritual. *The Christmas Eve: A Tale from the German* (Boston, 1843), a story by Christoph von Schmid but unattributed in this version, describes how

> all the family were busy, putting up and ornamenting the
> christmas [*sic*] tree. A young, beautiful fir tree with close
> branches, was placed in the parlor between two windows . . .
> hung [with] the little presents, beautiful fruits, various

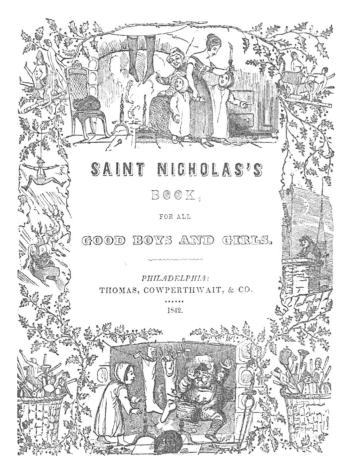

Figure 4 *Saint Nicholas's Book for All Good Boys and Girls* (Philadelphia, PA, 1842), title page – Baldwin Library, University of Florida – 23h47601

> colored sweetmeats, neat baskets full of sugared almonds,
> garlands of artificial flowers, ornamented with rose colored
> or sky blue ribbons, and a multitude of glittering beads,
> upon the branches and twigs of the tree; and then illumi-
> nated the tree with two dozen little lamps. (109–10)

The Christmas Tree (Boston, 1845; 1844) describes the life of Dr Charles
Follen, a German-born professor at Harvard: 'Every Christmas since
Charles was two years old, his father had dressed a Christmas-tree for
him, after the fashion of his own country' (3). Young Charles dreams of
a Christmas tree filled with Christian aphorisms: 'On one, for example,
was a representation of a kind and benevolent Quaker, surrounded by
a group of Indians, who gazed upon him with respect and affection. Then
came the motto: "BLESSED ARE THE PEACE-MAKERS"' (6). Here
the Christmas tree is carefully aligned with Christ's instruction and love –
with additional Western conquest – offering a justification for the newfangled practice. By 1846, it seems that Christmas trees are common
knowledge, almost tiresomely so:

> Most people have heard – perhaps till they have been tired –
> of the mode of celebrating Christmas eve in Germany; of the
> fir tree, with its numerous wax lights, and bunches of sweet-
> meats, and toys, and gaily coloured ribbons set upon the
> parlour, and the tables placed around the room with the
> names of all the members of the family, to which, somehow
> or other, all sorts of pretty things find their way.
>
> Sinnett, *A Story about a Christmas*, 1846, 1

The details that emerge about Christmas trees in this period show that they
are novelties, and often children's books included illustrations of how they
should look, as in Mrs Percy Sinnett's frontispiece (Figure 5).

A striking difference from today comes in Christmas tree placement upon
tables, and sometimes on objects set upon tables to make them even higher.
Sinnett details a triple-engineered tree stand: 'In the middle of the room stood
a large round table, and on the top of that a washing tub turned upside down . . .

THE CHRISTMAS TREE.

Figure 5 Mrs Percy Sinnett, *A Story about a Christmas in the Seventeenth Century* (London, 1846), frontispiece – Baldwin Library, University of Florida – 23h16771

and on top of that, in a large pot concealed by many frills and furbelows of pink, blue, and gilt paper, a young fir tree rising like a pyramid to the ceiling (*A Story about a Christmas*, 1846, 8). From the 1840s trees become a Christmas essential:

> The practice of hanging up stockings in the chimney corner
> for Kriss Kringle to fill with toys . . . for good children, and
> rods for naughty children, is being superseded by that of
> placing a Christmas Tree on the table to await the annual
> visit of the worthy Santa Klaus.
>
> *Kriss Kringle's Christmas Tree*, 1847, v

That initial vogue for trees has been preserved in texts for children ever since, often accompanied by stockings too, of course, as they resisted 'being superseded'.

Christmas, despite its growing association with childhood, presents, and family celebration, is not entirely fun and games in the 1840s. Even children's books sounded strong Christian reservations about the child-centric nature of shifting cultures of celebration. *A New Year's Gift: From the Children of the Warren Street Chapel. Boston, January 1, 1841* offers a short treatise on 'The Law of Christ', emphasising sombre behaviour: 'In the first place you can do much by taking care not to be troublesome; not to tease and interrupt other people, when they are busy, not to make a noise when they wish to be still' (4). The hubbub of expecting a 'gift', despite the title of this book, has no place in the holidays. Instead one might 'assist others; you can also quietly do much for them. You can take a part of their burdens on your shoulders and carry it' (6). The vogue for death narratives at Christmas also remains strong. *Elihu Lewis: or, The Fatal Christmas Day* (Boston, 1848) intends to offer a 'friendly caution' (8) against skating on thin ice by representing the death of the titular character, who 'was drowned, amidst the high enjoyments of a skating frolick' (9). At least in this case the book does not hide the death narrative in a chirpy seasonal title.

Christmas books in the 1840s also deploy the new modes of celebration as a tool for cultural othering. *Saint Nicholas's Book* (London, 1842)

Figure 6 *Christmas ABC* (Philadelphia, PA, and New York, 1844), cover –
Baldwin Library, University of Florida – 15p823

intertwines its *A Visit from St Nicholas* with a later story about 'Taj Mahal Agrah: A Story of Hindostan', setting foreign customs against newly established, quasi-religious Western ones.

Such othering can take nasty turns. In the innocuous-looking *Christmas ABC*, published in Philadelphia and New York in 1844, are illustrations, one letter per page, typical of alphabet books (Figure 6). Reflecting the casual racism of the time, N is for 'Ne-gro' appears in this list, with a picture of a black man who is smoking, sitting on a wall in what appears to be a shipyard. The picture is entirely incongruous with the other letters that have subject matter in keeping with childhood objects, like 'Grapes', 'House', and 'Trum-pet'. Some books from this period spend more effort in their attempts at othering. *The Annualette* (Boston, 1844) offers a lengthy story of 'Perdita, or the Chinese Foundling'. A Mrs Goldsmith finds an abandoned girl in Macao, near 'a spot where a large cross upon a stone pediment has been erected' (88). Christian symbolism continues in that the child is found 'partly concealed in the hedge which surrounded the cross, [in] a Chinese basket, which on examination, she found contained a female infant. She knew that the Chinese sometimes destroy or expose their female children to avoid the trouble and expense of bringing them up' (88–91). The girl unsurprisingly becomes a model of Christian living, and 'she continued to improve in mind and body, that she became a highly-educated woman, and a most amiable and attractive one' (97). The holiday moral here appears to be that with the correct Christian upbringing, any girl might 'improve'. British colonial settings are also investigated through children's Christmas books slightly later in the century. The *Boy's Own Annual: A Holiday Companion for All Seasons* (London, 1861) is concerned with Christmas 'Down South' in Australia, showcasing a fairly irreligious holiday of 'delight and festivity' (2) with gold hunters having 'the best parts of a kangaroo stuffed' (2) for dinner. Adventure stories had long considered the nations of the global south. In part these moments of cultural difference are products of that narrative trend. Yet it is also important to highlight how Christmas becomes a key element in cultural and racial division, because those divisions if anything can intensify over time, as Section 4 shows.

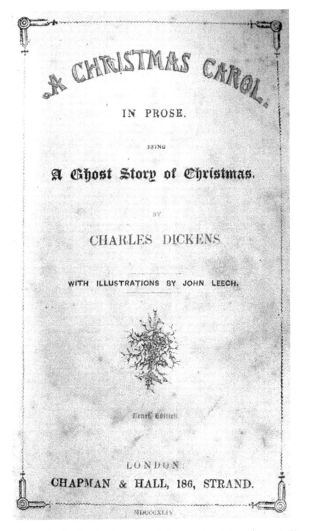

Figure 7 Charles Dickens, *A Christmas Carol* (London, 1843), title page of the tenth edition – Baldwin Library, University of Florida – 23h6926

The Charitable Christmas: Old versus New

These minor examples of Christmas books have not become canonical, but they do participate in circulating the traditions of Santa and stockings popularised by *A Visit from St Nicholas*. While Livingston's *A Visit from St Nicholas* comes to dominate American cultural practice, a book published two decades later is the most canonical children's Christmas text in Britain. Charles Dickens published *A Christmas Carol* in 1843 with Chapman and Hall on commission, in the hopes of financial success, as he owed money to his publishers (Schlicke, 'Chapman and Hall', 1999, 74). Although one might doubt whether *A Christmas Carol* is conceived as a children's book, it certainly becomes so in its subsequent history and must have been given to children as Christmas presents, with its canny publication date of 19 December 1843. The Baldwin Library's copy has a child-like ownership inscription for 'Mary Oshea Christmas Day 1843', showing how quickly the book could go from publisher, to shop, to buyer, and to recipient in this period.

A Christmas Carol elevates the format of the Christmas book beyond the typical production standards of the time. At 12 cm by 17 cm it is larger than most of the works considered so far. It also has colour illustrations by John Leech, and even the title page is printed in a festive red font. The frontispiece is careful to represent a multigenerational Christmas celebration with children and the elderly watching jolly adults cutting a caper. The only indications of holiday festivities are the Christmas greens. To the left of the image is a man grappling the neck of a wearily compliant young woman from behind while holding mistletoe, and more mistletoe hangs from the ceiling. To the right a man quaffs a tankard of ale.

The frontispiece (Figure 8) would seem to celebrate what Washington Irving describes as the 'old Christmas', and we later learn that it is the Christmas of Fezziwig, Scrooge's former employer. The large social gathering, with music, drink, and dancing, has no presents, no particular focus on family or children, and no Christmas tree or stockings. Instead of representing new modes of Christmas, Dickens harks back to older ones that emphasise community and charitable providing for the poor, particularly servants, employees, or local tradespeople. Dickens offers a complex

Figure 8 Charles Dickens, *A Christmas Carol* (London, 1843) – John Leech's illustration for the frontispiece – Baldwin Library, University of Florida – 23h6926

backlash against the increasing commercialisation of the holiday season, and also the heavy moralising in Christmas books that fetishise death and piety. In the end he also attacks some of the older holiday traditions, including one represented on this frontispiece.

Dickens' Christmas famously opens, instead of closes, with mortality – 'Marley was dead: to begin with' (1) – but its main focus is charity. In a part that is often reduced or cut in subsequent retellings for children, charitable collectors come to Scrooge's door and argue:

> At this festive season of the year, Mr. Scrooge . . . it is more than usually desirable that we should make some slight provision for the poor and destitute, who suffer greatly at the present time. Many thousands are in want of common necessaries; hundreds of thousands are in want of common comforts, sir. (12)

After first responding that there are debtors' prisons enough for them, Scrooge then replies that they might as well just die: 'they had better do it, and decrease the surplus population' (14). Of course the cruelty of the rich miser contrasts with the homely jollity of Bob Cratchit, who experiences the pleasures of a communal – and more importantly familial – holiday:

> The clerk . . . went down a slide on Cornhill, at the end of a lane of boys, twenty times, in honour of its being Christmas-eve, and then ran home to Camden Town as hard as he could pelt, to play at blindman's-buff. (18)

These two polar positions on Christmas are reconciled in favour of charity and family owing to supernatural spiritual intervention. Cratchit's family receive 'not the little prize Turkey: the big one!' (156), and Scrooge effectively joins the family, going from 'his melancholy dinner in his usual melancholy tavern' (18) to Tiny Tim's surrogate parent: 'He did it all, and infinitely more; and to Tiny Tim, who did NOT die, he was a second father' (165). Dickens pokes fun here at the charitable Christmas narratives that kill off protagonists. Importantly, the final message of

A Christmas Carol concerns the avoidance of alcohol. In the same paragraph as Tiny Tim's 'God bless Us, Every One!' we learn that Scrooge 'had no further intercourse with Spirits, but lived upon the Total Abstinence Principle, ever afterwards; and it was always said of him, that he knew how to keep Christmas well, if any man alive possessed the knowledge' (165–6). While emphasising sobriety, Dickens rejects the novelty of Santa, stockings, and trees – which make no appearance in his story – while 'presents' appear only once. At first Dickens seems to advocate an older form of Christmas celebration, one that centres very strongly around food. The Ghost of Christmas Present is depicted in a green robe, with onions and a sirloin of beef. The list of his holiday accoutrements includes: 'holly, mistletoe, red berries, ivy, turkeys, geese, game, poultry, brawn, meat, pigs, sausages, oysters, pies, puddings, fruit, and punch' (79–80). Note, however, that Dickens does not entirely justify such old bounty: the 'plenty of beer' provided by Fezziwig (51) becomes eschewed in favour of a modest 'bowl of smoking bishop' (Figure 9), a kind of mulled wine, by the end (164).

Jonathan Buckmaster highlights the movement from Fezziwig's huge party to the more modest celebration of Fred's house to the even smaller 'homely feast' of the Cratchits to show how in this work 'modesty has become the keynote' ('Ten Thousand Million Delights', 2015, 124). Dickens advocates a very limited bounty, despite the extra-large turkey, reflecting the idea that monetary charity should in fact supplant the older holiday open tables.

Charity, family, and sobriety are the keywords of the Dickensian Christmas. These ideals come to dominate the representation of the holidays in children's books for at least the remainder of the nineteenth century. If *A Visit from St Nicholas* is the most heavily illustrated poem in American literature, then *A Christmas Carol* is one of the most adapted and influential children's novels in British literature, beaten out as far as I have been able to determine only by *Alice's Adventures in Wonderland*.[7] Yet Dickens is not 'inventing' Christmas for children or adults.[8] In fact his

---

[7] For more on the story's afterlives, see Davis, *The Lives and Times of Ebenezer Scrooge*, 1990.

[8] See Standiford, *The Man Who Invented Christmas*, 2017; 2008.

Figure 9 Charles Dickens, *A Christmas Carol* (London, 1843) – John Leech's illustration of Scrooge serving a small cup of mulled wine, p. 164 – Baldwin Library, University of Florida – 23h6926

moderate line on celebrations would largely be ignored, as would his seemingly deliberate removal of children's presents, stockings, trees, and the other material goods that come to define the holiday. (His 'A Christmas Tree', an autobiographical story of 1850, covers much of that other ground.) Nonetheless, the book is continually rereleased in new versions, including for very young children, like *A Christmas Carol: Rewritten for Young Readers by Margaret Waters* (Chicago, 1907), which omits around half of the sentences, or *A Christmas Carol: A Pop-Up Book* (Baltimore, 1989), which is only 250 words long.

Old Christmases and New

Dickens' clever use of Christmases from the past, present, and future works to be nostalgic and anti-nostalgic at once. Christmas books for children around 1840 regularly have to negotiate such crossovers between old and new. Some elements, like the 'Christmas greens' of holly, ivy, and mistletoe, are carried over unwaveringly as ancient customs. Harriet Martineau's *Christmas Day* (1825) has a frontispiece of the female members of a household mounting the Christmas greens (Figure 10). Dress aside, the scene could easily be from 1925 or 2015, in Britain at least, although only the mistletoe survives in widespread use across America. Even the pro-Puritan William M. Thayer permits greens in his Christmas celebrations: 'An evergreen does not fade; it is always the same – green. And so Christ, in honor of whose birth the day is called "Christmas", will not change. He is immutable, unchangeable' (*Merry Christmas*, 1854, 55).

Other festive traditions prove more contentious. Food and drink become a regular target of seasonal reformers, yet they also have adherents, perhaps not surprisingly in the case of food, in children's books. From a US perspective, Eliza Leslie's collection, *The Gift: A Christmas and New Year's Present for* 1839 (Philadelphia, PA, 1838), strongly advocates the consumption of eggnog in the story 'Poll Preble'. A rather old-fashioned uncle 'comes well armed with eggs and cream, for the egg-nog of the next day, a good old Virginia custom, from "below the ridge", which the old man would consider it a sacrilege to omit' (100). British author Louis Alexis Chamerovzow celebrates the communal open table, without the associations of feudalism, in *The Yule Log: For*

CHRISTMAS DAY.

Figure 10 Harriet Martineau, *Christmas Day* (London, 1825), frontispiece –
Baldwin Library, University of Florida – 15h1044

Everybody's Christmas Hearth (London, 1847). When it comes time for Abel, a woodcutter, and his wife to host the local Christmas banquet, they provide:

> a whole ham, with a bran-new [*sic*], rough, brown coat of raspings; and round the knuckle, a dashing, white paper-frill . . . neat's tongues . . . giant round of boiled beef, the top slice temptingly cut away, shewing the meat so pink and juicy . . . a roast sirloin, too, off some mammoth ox . . . pickled cabbage, pickled onions, pickled walnuts, piccalilli, and all sorts of pickles . . . a mountain of cheese. (48–9)

Abel is shocked by the expense of these provisions: 'What be thee going to do wi' all they wittles?' (50), he asks his wife, Beck, complaining that the feast will put them in 'the poor-huss, Beck; the Union!' (52). But she explains, 'Isn't it our turn to burn the Yule Log?' (51), and has herself, over time, saved enough money for the feast (56). The fantasy story continues to explain the mythical power of the yule log to bring good fortune and communal favour, validating the old Christmas customs of shared board. *Aunt Fanny's Christmas Stories* (New York, 1848) similarly details the season's lavish repast, with a child-centred approach:

> The children did not care for soup. Then they had a fish stuffed with all sorts of things, and stewed, and all the grown people said the fish was very nice; but the little ones did not care for that either. Then they had some roast beef and a boiled turkey with oysters. The children took all the turkey. . . . But this was not half the good things, for they afterwards had some delicious game, such as partridges, and woodcocks, and some fried oysters. All this pleased the grown people most. The children saved their appetites for the dessert. . . . It was a great plum-pudding all on fire! . . . After that there came ice-cream, and jellies, and sweetmeats. . . . Then the servants put on the table what the children liked best of all, and that was a dish of fine mottoes, and oranges and grapes and other nice fine fruits. (11–13)

Bridging the old Christmas traditions with the new, *Aunt Fanny* shows how communal indulgences can suit both, quite separate, tastes of children and adults. These separate expectations are considered across the following two sections. Sweetmeats aside, one of the key movements over this early period of children's Christmas texts, and a part of the childification of the holiday itself, is a rejection of the quasi-Bakhtinian ribaldry of earlier traditions. As Mrs Sinnett argues: 'We cannot agree with those who are inclined to mourn, as a sort of national calamity, the decay of old Christmas pastimes . . . we cannot sometimes help feeling that they are rather foolish and rather coarse' (*Story about a Christmas*, 1846, 3).

By considering these sometimes 'foolish and . . . coarse' foundations of the genre, this section has traced the significant cultural and religious ideals within early Christmas books for children. With the exceptions of tankards of ale and oysters, perhaps, all of these traditions are found in greater or lesser degrees in such books up to the present day. Yet such thematic consistency belies several changes to the market itself. The books are to become more ostentatious and carefully crafted, and in fact more Christmassy, as the following sections show.

2 The Moral Christmas, 1850–1910

This section considers the broadening of the book gift market that took place in the period from 1850 to 1910, and especially how these books are pitched to the adult buyer, often through prefatory material and advertisements, but also through overtly moralising content. It traces a continued strand of shared nostalgia, whereby intergenerational negotiations of the holidays are mediated through children's books, usually for the purposes of instruction. Also found in this period is a formidable Christian backlash against the supposedly new materialism, with a greater focus on Jesus' nativity and charity. Finally, this section considers the material text itself, and how Christmas gift books become enhanced by lavish printing and binding, contributing to a more effusive gift market.

The organising framework for separating this section and the next is somewhat specious: adultism or aetonormativity means that most, if not all, children's literature in some degree takes the perspective of older people.[9] There will invariably be crossovers in content, and many elements of Christmas, like the mounting of greens or decorating of the Christmas tree, seem equally to delight (or at least to employ) the young and old. Nonetheless adultism or childlike perspectives are often easy to delimit. The changing traditions can invest texts of this period with heavy nostalgia that only adults might feel, for instance. Similarly, the sadness in Washington Irving's *Old Christmas* lament, 'I am apt to think the world was more homebred, social, and joyous than at present' (1876, 1), could hardly register to a child's experience. In terms of collections of materials by other authors, the frequency of the poems of Robert Herrick in children's Christmas collections shows an adult editorial perspective attempting to recover older traditions and to expose young readers to canonical works. Books also begin to promote active community engagement – for the young and old – especially through charity and giving. Martha J. Lamb's *Merry Christmas* (Boston, 1870), for instance, insists that giving to the poor is considerably more seasonal than receiving one's own gifts. These contentions over the purpose of the holidays make children's books interventionist, at a wider cultural level, towards a reshaping of Christmas itself. The moralising Christmas book eventually loses ground to books emphasising fun, but in the nineteenth century, at least, such didacticism peppers the gift market.

Firstly, it is important to note that a somewhat cynical culture of offering a random hodgepodge of printed material in festive wrapping continues throughout this period. The content of such collections is often driven by the fact that moral stories, about Christmas or not, provide the bulk of children's literature from which a compiler might select. It is not until Lewis Carroll's *Alice's Adventures in Wonderland* (London, 1865) that a fantasy text supposedly 'unburdened by any moral whatsoever' might become widely celebrated.[10]

---

[9] See Nikolajeva, *Power, Voice and Subjectivity in Literature for Young Readers*, 2010.
[10] See chapter 2 of Jaques and Giddens, *Lewis Carroll's* Alice's Adventures in Wonderland *and* Through the Looking-Glass, for a discussion of *Alice* and morals, including this quotation from a review in *The Literary Churchman*.

Sometimes in Christmas collections it is difficult to find an organising principle, so the contents, be they moral or otherwise, might have been chosen fairly randomly. Often books make their hurried assembly apparent, like *Gems Gathered in Haste: A New Year's Gift for Sunday Schools* (Boston, 1851). The preface notes that 'on the 24th of December, 1850, a letter came to me from a friend, asking if I was preparing a tract, as in former days, for a New Year's Gift. ... I consulted the printer, and he agreed to do all he could' (np). Predictably, *Gems Gathered in Haste* collects random stories with no narrative through-line and no connection to the holiday season. This description could apply to many books seeking to take advantage of the holiday marketplace. *The Violet: A Christmas and New Year's Gift* (New York, 1858) has excellent engravings, but only three mundane stories of mild adventure. Another text with strong illustrations but otherwise atrocious content is George E. and Myra Sargent's *The Holly Tree: A Winter Gift* (London, 1850). The attractive skating scene in the frontispiece (Figure 11) and an initial poem called 'The Holly Tree' that makes almost no effort – 'Hurrah for the Holly! At Christmas tide / We'll deck with its berries our bright fire-side' (2) – seem intended to trick the adult buyer into seeing it as an appropriate holiday gift. The Baldwin Library copy has a gift inscription – 'Annie Elizabeth Morgan from Uncle Tom Xmas 1857' – indicating that it had languished seven years between publication and gifting. For the most part this section traces adultism and morality in books that more directly represent Christmas festivities, instead of making mere mention of them in titles.

Sometimes these works will sit oddly with contemporary notions of Christmas. Miss Planché's *The Santa Claus Annual: A Christmas and New Year's Gift* (New York, c.1876), for instance, mixes an apparent concern for jolly Santa in the title with a frontispiece illustration called 'The Bereaved' depicting a mourning widow holding a young baby. The discussion to follow attempts to situate such dour Christmas cultures within a children's seasonal gift market that makes more effort to entice buyers and readers.

Adultism

Some Christmas books make their appeal to adults apparent from their very title. Mrs Coleman's *The Mother's Present: A Holiday Gift for the Young*

Figure 11 George E. and Myra Sargent, *The Holly Tree: A Winter Gift* (London, 1850), frontispiece – Baldwin Library, University of Florida – 23h16242

(Boston, 1847), for instance, knowingly takes the perspective of a maternal buyer, even offering a printed gift page, detailing the expected 'to' and 'from', implying that a child could not buy it for himself or herself. Other books have prefaces clearly designed to give the wink, or indeed the authority, to adults. William M. Thayer's *Merry Christmas, a Christmas Present for Children and Youth* (Boston, 1854), for instance, points to the ignorance of children, which his book will repair:

> Children and youth know very little about the origin, design, and history of Christmas. They welcome it as a holiday while they are ignorant of its meaning. This volume is designed to instruct them upon these points, as well as to expose the superstitious notions, and unwise and foolish sayings and doings, connected with the celebration of this day. (v)

This address to adults makes clear that instruction will supersede any occasion for fun or celebration. *Christmas Blossoms and New Year's Wreath* (Boston, 1847), a lengthy hard-bound tome with fourteen stories and poems for older readers, again addresses parental buyers in its 'Advertisement' at the beginning of the book: 'Parents will discover in this book no false positions to pervert the judgment of their offspring, and no intense excitements tending to render them, in after life, the unhappy victims of a diseased imagination' (iii–iv). The anti-festive tone could not be clearer, making Christmas a plague that should be purged from young bodies and spirits.

More typically Christmas books around mid-century coat such bitter pills with a little sugar, and appeal to adult buyers and readers through more subtle mechanisms. Susan Pindar's *Fireside Fairies: Or Christmas at Aunt Elsie's* (New York, 1850) explains, in that long-standing justification for children's stories, how instruction can come through entertainment:

> There exists, in the minds of some parents, a strong and reasonable prejudice against Fairy Tales for children; as the extravagant imagery and improbable incidents, in which

they generally abound, often mislead or bewilder the youthful imagination. . . .

The mind of a child is easily impressible through the
medium of fancy; and this humble attempt to deck familiar,
yet important truths, and the home duties of every-day life,
in the drapery of fairy land, may, perhaps, serve to awaken
a reasoning thought, leading to an active principle. (5–6)

Similarly, *Holiday Stories with Many Pictures* (New York, 1850) brings in
generally merry tales and illustrations, but mixes in educational sections like
'The Parts of Speech' (94–6), usefully discussing interjections, nouns,
adjectives, verbs, pronouns, conjunctions, prepositions, adverbs, and arti-
cles, alongside a historical section on 'The Battle of Concord' (104–5).

At other times children's Christmas books have sections plainly
intended for the adult reader. Robert B. Brough's *A Cracker Bon-Bon
for Christmas Parties: Consisting of Christmas Pieces, for Private
Representation, and Other Seasonable Matter, in Prose and Verse*
(London, 1852) offers a heavily illustrated collection of entertainments,
mostly non-seasonal like 'King Alfred and the Cakes' and 'William
Tell'. The one piece of Christmas content is a carol rendering 'Oh,
rest you, merry gentlemen!' to consider the disquiet caused by paying
for seasonal celebrations (81–4). A Christmas 'tree' (Figure 12) is
made up of a pyramid of 'Bad Debts' (81).

Sometimes adultism is fun and not moral, as with Brough. The inclusion
of Robert Herrick usually signals the enjoyable side of an adult Christmas,
as in Julia C. R. Dorr's *Santa Claus Souvenir* (New York, 1882), which
quotes Herrick:

> Drink now the strong beere,
> Cut the white loaf here
> The while the meate is a-shredding
> For the rare mince pie,
> And the plums stand by
> To fill the paste that's a-kneading. (9)

Figure 12 Robert B. Brough, *A Cracker Bon-Bon for Christmas Parties* (London, 1852), p. 81 – Baldwin Library, University of Florida – 23h4895

In these cases the collections are intended to please young and old, as made plain by the title of *Christmas Bowers Sparkling with the Brightest Gems from the Mines of Literature . . . For Boys and Girls and Older Folk* (Philadelphia, PA, 1892).

Nostalgia

Nostalgia is inevitably an adult experience, but it is not necessarily a lived one. It is a fetishisation of supposed olden times that exists simply because 'we like to read of what they used to do at Christmas in the centuries past' (*Christmas Bowers*, 1892, 22). Washington Irving's 1819 *Sketch Book* is an early instance of this expression – it becomes packaged for children and re-illustrated by Randolph Caldecott in *Old Christmas: From the Sketch Book of Washington Irving* (London, 1876). The fifty-year gap pushes anything discussed by Irving outside of most readers' living memory, even if Irving's insistence on the importance of roast beef, ale, wassailing, and fireside storytelling has great longevity in books for adults and children. In its insistence on the communal instead of the familial (Figure 13), however, it very much bucks against the real Christmas experience of late nineteenth-century children. The old Christmas of adults, where 'each tavern is enlivened with the sound of a fiddle, and the heavy tramping which accompanies it informs us of a rustic dance: the home-made elder-wine circulates merrily', slowly yields to a family-focused and child-centric one (*History of the Christmas Festival*, 1843, 70).

It seems that much of the nostalgia in children's Christmas books is meant as a counter to the over-Puritanical backlash against newer modes of celebration, including an obsession with teetotalism. Hezekiah Butterworth's *The Christmas Book* (Boston, 1891) represents the Puritans of the English Civil War as spoiling the fun: 'Silent Christmasses were proclaimed in the Protectorate of Cromwell. The festival was altogether abolished, and the display of the emblems of the Nativity was held to be seditious' (87). Butterworth also points out that America's first Puritans are in fact keen to celebrate Christmas properly, quoting from *Chronicles of the Pilgrims* to record this entry from the Mayflower voyage: 'Monday the 25th, being Christmas Day, we began to drink water aboard, but at night the Master caused us to have some Beere, and so on board we had diverse times now and then some Beere, but on shore none at all' (98). The message is clear: even the true Protestants fleeing religious persecution in England thought beer appropriate for the festive season.

While alcohol might or might not feature in recollections of former Christmases, certainly food continues to be a ubiquitous topic. *Christmas Bowers*, a mixed collection of holiday materials including 'Christmas in Ye Olden Time', recalls that 'in the country an English gentleman always invited all his neighbors and tenants to his great hall at daybreak on Christmas morning. There they were regaled upon toast, sugar nutmeg

" Never did Christmas board display a more goodly and gracious assemblage of countenances."—
PAGE 123.

Figure 13 Washington Irving, *The Old Christmas*, illust. Randolph Caldecott (London, 1876), p. 122 – Baldwin Library, University of Florida – 23h19542

and good old Cheshire cheese' (22). While the recipes of *Christmas Bowers* are somewhat idiosyncratic, the head of a boar makes frequent appearances in children's festive books. *Christmas Sports and Other Stories* (Boston, 1855) includes a boar's head as its frontispiece. T. B. Murray's *Christmas-Tide, and Its Customs* (New York, 1860) notes that the 'soused Boar's Head . . . was carried to the principal table in the hall, with great solemnity, as the first dish on Christmas-day' (14). Perhaps because Murray's book is sponsored by the General Protestant Episcopal Sunday School Union, there is no mention of alcohol at these ancient feasts. Nostalgia can be put to a variety of uses in this period, including conservative and, surprisingly, liberal ones, but either way the grounds of debate, particularly concerned as they are with alcohol and offal, connect to adult modes of Christmas celebration. The following sections consider how the more novel forms of festivity, including Santa Claus and Christmas trees, could be similarly manipulated.

Santa Claus: Exposed and Rejected

Some thirty years after the invention of Santa Claus, books deploy the saint for a variety of moral or adultist purposes. For the most part the distinction between the American Santa Claus (or Kriss Kringle, or Saint Nicholas) as the emergent gift bringer and the English Father Christmas as the ancient presider over more adult festivities remains intact. In the discussion to follow, I focus on Santa Claus, simply because he is associated more strongly with children's books until the end of the nineteenth century.[11]

Sometimes Kriss Kringle is lambasted for being distinctively unsaintly, if not sacrilegious. William M. Thayer offers one of the strongest attacks, representing a foolish man who permits his children to believe in Santa:

> It was quite pleasing to him to see his children enjoy the hoax about Santaclaus coming down the chimney. He would say and do almost anything to confirm their belief in the

---

[11] For a discussion of distinctions and overlaps between Santa Claus and Father Christmas, see Armstrong, 'England and German Christmas', 2008.

strange feat. He did not mean any harm, but, like a great
many people, *he did not think.*

Merry Christmas, 1854, 32

Some authors argue that a belief in Santa is especially harmful to poor
children, who have little hope of full stockings. Susan Warner's *Carl
Krinken: His Christmas Stocking* (New York, 1854) states laconically:
'Indeed it may be noted as a fact, that the Christmas of poor children has
but little of his care' (12).[12] Elizabeth Wetherell's adaptation of Warner's
story around 1900 explains more fully: 'I am afraid there will be many
whose fathers and mothers have never thought of making arrangements for
the visit of Santa Claus, and unless Santa Claus is made welcome, he never
comes' (Warner, *Christmas Stocking*, c.1900, np). Yet the knowing reader's
realisation about the absence of Santa should nonetheless provoke
a charitable desire to replace him: 'It is a rather sad little story, in some
ways, but it is none the worse for that, if it should make you, when you read
it, think a little of poor little boys' (np). Santa's inability to help the poor is
also explored in Joanna H. Mathews' *Elsie's Santa Claus* (New York, 1876).
Elsie's family are poor, so she is told that 'Santa Claus will not come to us
tonight' (49); it is all owing to her father: 'He had been a careless, impro-
vident man. . . . Moreover, he was of a roving, unsettled disposition, which
led him from place to place, thereby depriving his children of a permanent
home, and also preventing them from forming any reliable or lasting
friendships' (53). Ultimately Elsie's new friends supply some modest presents when 'Santa Claus' otherwise neglects her. Lizzie Lawson and Robert
Ellice Mack's *Christmas Roses* (New York, c.1886) has a little poem about
Santa not visiting poor children:

> 'I don't believe that Santa Clause will come to you and me,'
> Said little crippled Nell, 'a'cause, we are so poor you see'. (np)

---

[12] The Baldwin Library copy offers an interesting example of holiday gifting and
regifting, with two inscriptions: 'Master L. K. Worster from his Mother
24.12.1853' and 'C. S. Worster from his Brother 4 Jany 1860'.

Susie M. Waring's *Diamonds and Rubies; or The Home of Santa Claus* (New York, 1864) is an early imagining of Santa in the North Pole. Waring reverses the idea that Santa cares little for the poor, by representing him as hosting 'hungry wayfarers – for the house of Santa Claus is ever open to such' (19). Santa in fact teaches the protagonist, Brenda, religion and charity, because 'however fortunate you may think Brenda, she yet lacked the most precious thing of all – the gift from heaven, which no man can give or take away' (10). Waring takes advantage of naughty-or-nice tropes to ensure that all of the presents do not lead to selfishness, showing pre-redemption Brenda as 'too busy thinking how she should find out the "best thing" in New-York, to stop for the little, cracked, bleeding hand [of a poor waif], held out to her' (13). This connection between Santa and giving even leads one author to re-emphasise the sanctified origins of St Nicholas. Mary H. Seymour in *Mollie's Christmas Stocking* (Boston, 1869) has Daisy, the youngest daughter, ask her mother in baby talk: '"is Santa Kaus 'Our Father who art in Heaven?'" "Yes, Daisy," said her mamma, "God puts it into our hearts to do these kind things for each other, and you know we keep Christmas-day in remembrance of God's best gift to us – His own beloved Son"' (18). The text also exposes the performance of Santa in having an older boy, Edward, split the gift distribution duties with his mother: 'I think you had better enact Santa Claus to-night; so you go and hold court in the dining-room, and if there is any thing to fall to your share, I'll stay here in the parlor, and take charge of it' (11). Such relatively genial depictions of the work of Santa are far more common than those condemning him.

Adultist representations of Santa in fact often deploy him as a fairly benign figure for moral messages or, like *Mollie's Christmas Stocking*, break the rule against exposing him for a fraud. For George P. Webster's *Santa Claus and His Works* (New York, *c.*1872), which represents Santa and his team producing toys, a key component in the success of the saint is his abstinence and his work ethic:

> He never was known to drink brandy or wine;
> But day after day at his bench he is found,
> For he works for good children hard, all the year round. (np)

HANDS THAT TREMBLED, AS EVERYBODY COULD SEE

Figure 14 Kate Douglas Wiggin, *The Romance of a Christmas Card* (Boston and New York, 1916) – Baldwin Library, University of Florida – 23h37435

Rather like the odd moment at the end of *A Christmas Carol* when Scrooge goes dry, Santa teaches children that good people do not touch alcohol. More often an adultist perspective comes through the assertion that Santa does not exist. The children of S. P. Doughty's *Playing Santa Claus, and Other Christmas Tales* (Boston, 1865) take on Santa's role themselves when they note, matter-of-factly, that 'there is not really any such person as Santa Claus. It is our father and mother, and other kind friends, who fill our stockings' (8–9). In a later story in the collection, 'A Dream', a little girl gives her drunken father a Bible, and he 'promised never to drink again, and he had good work, and they could all live comfortably' (86), again showing the strange association between Santa collections and temperance.

Exposing Santa in children's books is typically associated with children coming of age. Una Locke and Frances Lee's *Holiday Tales* (Boston, 1863) is published by the American Tract Society. The children in the story 'Holidays at Mr. Lancaster's' explicitly place themselves as too old for Santa: 'Oh, we've become too large for stockings and Santa Claus. ... We hung up our stockings last Christmas, but this year mamma said she would make a new arrangement, and we should receive our presents after dinner' (28). In Cousin Mary's *Christmas Holidays at Chestnut Hill* (Boston, *c*.1853), the poem 'Who Was Santa-Claus' includes the reveal:

> It seemed to puzzle little heads,
> None wiser than the other;
> Till Julia clapped her hands and cried,
> 'O, Santa-Claus was *mother!*' (168)

In a slightly later period we see the development of the communal Santa – whereby a local aged gentleman dresses up for children across multiple families. Kate Douglas Wiggin's *The Romance of a Christmas Card* (Boston and New York, 1916) gives a good sense of the performative qualities necessary in putting on the crimson costume:

> There was a momentary fear that John Trimble, a pillar of
> prohibition, might have imbibed hard cider; so gay, so
> nimble, so mirth-provoking was Santa Claus. When was

John Trimble ever known to unbend sufficiently to romp up
the side aisle jingling his sleigh bells, and leap over a front
pew stuffed with presents, to gain the vantage-ground he
needed for the distribution of his pack? (114–15)

Wiggin's Santa distributes gifts in the local church, while congregants
disclose a familiar fear that Christmas, especially Santa's Christmas, and
alcohol should not mix. It seems like fears over a drunk Santa are long-
standing ones.

Father Christmas in the period 1850–1910 is characteristically associated
with benevolence and childhood joy, as the following section explores, but
it is important to register the significant backlash against him in authors who
wish to explore a more serious holiday, or even those who take the older
perspective that he must be excised or uncovered as a performance.
Tellingly, publishers are willing to capitalise on children's fondness for
Santa, through titles and frontispiece illustrations, even for anti-Santa
content.

Newfangled Christmas Trees

Christmas trees received similar moral appropriations from the 1850s,
becoming strongly associated with Christ. The Christmas tree, perhaps
more easily than Santa Claus, could physically embody allegories of
Christendom. The General Protestant Episcopal Sunday School Union
published *A Christmas Tree for Christ's Children*, for instance, in
New York in 1860. The frontispiece (Figure 15) of this book signals its
thematic intention by representing a tree with a model of a church at the top,
where an angel or star might go today, and a family with seated girls, open
Bibles in hand, with father and son standing to oversee festivities. But there
is something very odd about this tree: 'The Tree was a real growing orange-
tree, which Mr. Oldham had had brought in from the conservatory, and had
real oranges growing upon it' (8). The children are disappointed to eat
'nasty and sour' oranges (11), but they learn that bitter citrus is 'just like
a man in his natural state; he only bears bad fruit, for he only does things
that do not please God' (12). Upon closer inspection, the tree has a serpent,

Front.   Christmas Tree,

Figure 15 *Christmas Tree for Christ's Children* (New York, 1860), frontispiece –
Baldwin Library, University of Florida – 23h5969

with Bible verses designed to remind the children of the fall (15–17). The next forty pages explore the morals behind additional tree-mounted verses. Although the children of the story do not express much disappointment, the bitter orange Christmas tree understandably did not become popular.

A similar attempt at moralising through the Christmas tree comes in H. S. E.'s *The Marleigh Christmas Tree, and What Came of It. A Story for School-Girls* (London, *c*.1870s), published by the Society for Promoting Christian Knowledge. The Rectory hosts its first Christmas tree, festooned with elaborate decorations 'ordered from Germany' (11). Every local child receives a small gift from the tree, and they play games, sing carols, and are given 'a bun to carry home' (13). Before the children leave, however, the Rector warns them that the tree should teach them kindness towards their impending death and judgement: 'And so will your Christmas Tree have borne golden fruit, which will be stored up for you [in Heaven] against the great day of account' (15). The rest of the narrative reveals the various ways in which the children perform good deeds as a result of the Christmas tree lesson. Although the exact mechanics are less clear, the connection between the tree and potential brimstone is similar to that of the Episcopal version. Theodore Parker makes his emphasis on Christian lessons apparent from the title of his *The Two Christmas Celebrations*, *A. D. I and MDCCLV* (Boston, 1859). This topical book parallels the two Christmases to oppose oppression:

> Such wicked men killed Jesus, just as . . . our Protestant fathers hung the Quakers and whipped the Baptists; or as the Slaveholders in the South now . . . whip a man to death who insists on working for himself and his family, and not merely for men who only steal what he earns. (13)

Parker's modern communal celebration will feature 'above all a Christmas Tree. There shall be gifts on it for all the children under twelve' (29). Although many in the community oppose racial integration, the text makes a point of saying that position is unchristian: 'That will be a *Christian* Christmas, – not a Heathen Christmas. . . . I want the *poor ones*, too. . . . I don't know that I like colored folks particularly, but I think God does, or he would not have colored 'em' (34). Although it is not exactly a ringing call for equality, the tree becomes central to showing how all children should be brought together for celebration.

Inclusive texts like Parker's are unfortunately rare. More typical are attacks on Christmas trees as newfangled, as part of an adult position that simply opposes holiday innovation. As Neil Armstrong argues, '"serious" Christians were beginning to realign the Christmas tree with a secular commercial Christmas which could readily be contrasted with an ideal of simple rustic piety' ('England and German Christmas', 2008, 496). Caroline E. K. Davis' *A Christmas Story* (Boston, 1868) represents Mrs Leroyd, an uppity community member who queries the absence of a Christmas tree in the home of her poor employee, calling it 'quite an old fashion' (58). The central boy of the story later concludes: 'I'd give more for old Santa Claus than for all the Christmas-trees in the world' (93). It is telling here that by 1868 trees can be seen as novel, while Santa is traditional. Absolutely central to the story of Christmas is forgetting, or manufacturing, the history of the holiday. Martha J. Lamb's *Merry Christmas* (Boston, 1870) similarly rejects the tree, with protagonists who

> had never had a Christmas-tree, but adhered to the good old stocking fashion. Grandmamma had told the children that Santa Claus didn't like to be bothered with hanging things on trees! (168–9)

For the bulk of this period those giving presents had to decide whether they should be on a tree or in a stocking. The texts discussed earlier in this Element go further in associating the tree with heavy moralising or dismissing it as a novelty. Despite these minor hold-backs, the Christmas tree is largely seen as essential to Christmas by adults and children alike, which is why it occurs so frequently in the titles of books from this period.

Christmas Charity

It is unsurprising, perhaps, given the fame of *A Christmas Carol*, that children's Christmas books are obsessed with charity. This obsession applies, in some subtly different ways, on both sides of the Atlantic. The new culture of giving presents to children within the family had a danger of sidelining older modes of communal giving. Children's authors are careful to remind children of the need to give, not receive, sometimes going so far as to encourage children to abstain from their own presents.

Children rarely are given *nothing* in the narratives of the period, but often small gifts are regifted to even poorer children. In Annie S. Swan's *Katie's Christmas Lesson* (Edinburgh, c.1880), Katie receives a disappointing stocking:

> Some fruit, and nuts, and sweets, and down in the toe
> a bright new silver shilling – that was all. Not a doll nor
> a toy of any kind. So, in a fit of temper, Katie pushed all the
> things on to the floor . . . and, laying her head down on the
> pillow, cried for very vexation. (35)

Katie's mother informs her that they are too poor for expensive gifts, and more importantly: 'This is Christmas Day! . . . Don't you remember this is the birthday of Jesus Christ, who was so meek and lowly and unselfish' (36). Katie's fortunes turn around and she learns to be more generous of spirit in the end. Although there is no story to match the illustration, *Christmas Joys*, a collection published in Chicago in 1899, has a striking picture of what happens when a stocking is empty on Christmas day (Figure 16).

Empty-handed children are meant to learn the importance of giving over receiving. Such messages often come through representations of either Scrooge-like tight-fistedness or children's benevolence. James T. Brady goes with the former in *A Christmas Dream* (New York, 1860). This distinctly odd book depicts 'a ragged and barefooted girl' (8), who 'had not yet become acquainted with Adam Smith's Wealth of Nations' (9). A gentleman refuses to give her money, 'Not one cent, I say – begone!' (7), and she ends up being crushed by his carriage. The horrific scene is intended, I suppose, to demonstrate the evils of denying holiday charity. Another rich miser is M. E. Braddon's character Sir John Penlyon in *The Christmas Hirelings* (London, 1894). He detests the 'overwhelming shower

Figure 16 *Christmas Joys* (Chicago, 1899), np – Baldwin Library, University of Florida – 39h117

of stationery in the shape of pamphlets, booklets, circulars, and reports of every imaginable kind of philanthropic scheme for extracting money from the well-to-do classes' (23).

Santa is deployed again for charitable purposes, but this time including self-denial, in Belle and Martin Towne's *Santa Claus' Dream, a Christmas Cantata for the Use of Sunday-Schools* (Chicago, 1894). A Little Girl tells St Nicholas:

> Now Santa, I want to tell you what *I* know. I know
> a Sunday-school where we have *no* Christmas tree at all,
> for ourselves. But oh! the good things we gather for the
> poor! We just follow your example, Santa, and give, and
> give, and our hearts grow warmer, and our hearts grow
> larger, the more we give. (25)

There is a strong strain of teaching children, even those believing in Santa,
not to expect gifts. Sometimes this message is hard-won. In *A Christmas
Time by 'Pansy'* (Boston, 1875) children take a sleigh ride with all of their
presents, but when the sleigh tips over the presents are lost – except for
those of one child, Willis, who had used his Christmas money to give to the
poor (19). Raymond MacDonald Alden's *Why the Chimes Rang*
(Indianapolis, IN, 1909) tells of two young country boys who wish nothing
more than to donate to the town church; when one manages to do so, the
bells ring of their own accord. Charlotte O'Brien's *The Cottagers' Christmas*
(London, 1856) describes an extended poverty tour as part of Christmas
festivities:

> I am going to visit many poor people to-day, whom
> God has not thought fit to bless with wealth, as he had
> done you. You will see little children who often know
> what it is to want a dinner, who have frequently not
> clothes sufficient to shield them from the cold. All these
> sights will be new and painful to you, but you will see
> bright sides even to these gloomy pictures. I shall be
> able to show you a contented mind, making even the
> poorest home a place of happiness; a spirit of unselfish-
> ness and affection shining through the miseries of sick-
> ness and want; and above all, I think I shall be able to
> prove to you, before you return home, that it really is
> 'more blessed to give than to receive'. (8)[13]

---

[13] The same biblical quotation ends *Alice's Watch: A Christmas Story* (*c*.1870s).

O'Brien goes on to detail a poor old couple who are given potatoes for Christmas; they in turn share their meal with an even poorer neighbour. As this litany of examples attests, children are continually shown the need to donate presents or food for orphans or the elderly.

Equally strong is the idea of regifting. Margaret Vandegrift's *Holidays at Home: For Boys and Girls* (Philadelphia, PA, 1882) includes an object lesson called 'The Travels of a Christmas Tree', in which a poor family cannot afford a tree, so the seller gives it to them for free (70); they in turn pass the tree to a poor older woman on the floor below, who passes away, with 'dying eyes [that] grew strangely bright as the little tree twinkled before them' (78). Oliver Optic's *The Christmas Gift. A Story for Little Folks* (Boston, 1863) has little Flora gather 'up the books, games, and pictures that belonged to her' to exchange them for 'all the money they cost, so that she could give it to poor Mrs. White' (57). However, when her brother tries to give money to a beggar, his father reprimands him: 'Those who have any thing to give away ought to be very careful to whom they give it. The man looked like a drunkard' (72). Although those with genuine need may be given Christmas charity, children are advised to be alert to scam artists. A corollary message is that the poor should make their own charity. In *Christmas Greens*, published in Philadelphia (*c*.1865) by the American Sunday-School Union, poverty is beaten by hard work, not charity. That there are undeserving and deserving poor, abstaining from drink and working hard, is a strong American inflection within the genre. The children complain that there will be 'no Christmas dinner at all?' (9), while their mother explains, 'we have only just money enough to pay our rent' (10). They set to 'go out to the cedar swamp and get some evergreens, and then mother and you can go to work and make some wreaths, and we can sell them to folks and get some money and buy some-thing' (19), and, indeed, they earn a merry Christmas.

A focus on charity and the Christmases of the poor is so prevalent that an entire book could be written on this topic alone. It becomes the most common motif in the second half of the nineteenth century, and the general thrust of the moral, in both Britain and America, is largely not altered across the period. In fact, it tends to be one-note: children receiving gifts occasion anxiety because there is almost no good deed associated with their reward. As *The Christmas Party* (London, *c*.1850) succinctly puts it: 'self-conceit and vanity [are] well punished' (24), but this lesson must come through the rejection of gifts and a new emphasis on giving, at times to the sacrifice of children's presents as a form of self-abnegation. The birch rod of St Nicholas is long forgotten.

Dying for Christmas

Death is an almost ubiquitous topic in children's Christmas books from 1850 to 1910, with eighty-three works in the Baldwin library concerned with Christmas death over this period. Unlike modern uses of death as a Christmas joke, for example Elmo and Patsy Trigg Shropshire's song 'Grandma Got Run Over by a Reindeer' (1979), mortality in the nineteenth century signals the need for Christ's salvation. Although Maria Nikolajeva argues that the persistent incidence of 'separation, death and grief' in children's fiction tends to be 'introduced in diluted forms' (*Reading for Learning*, 2014, 83), these Christmas books do not sugar-coat the representation of dying.

Even at the time death stories are seen as a little heavy-handed for children. In Davis' *A Christmas Story* (1868) a death ballad leads a child to exclaim, '"Now, I call that too horrid bad for a Christmas story!" ... brushing his hand across his eyes, while the little girls and Arthur made no pretence of hiding their tears' (24–5). Yet death can be seen as a necessary part of reflecting on the meaning of the season. In *Christmas Hours* (Boston, 1859), a family attends a Christmas Eve sermon to learn:

> Many of you, my young friends, are anticipating with gladness the festivities of the morrow. ... But have you thought of a more certain celebration, a larger and more joyous Christmas gathering, a more emphatic and happy welcome, in store for each and all? This day – this week – before the old year closes, some of you may be called to that larger reunion of friends and home. But are you making the needed preparation? (22)

Child death at Christmas, as this preacher warns, is a great risk in these narratives. Often a dying child is seemingly tacked onto the end of the story. Edward Rand's *Christmas Jack* (New York, 1878) kills off Elsie

Grace, a little girl in the neighbourhood, noting in the final sentence: 'And so through the shadows of death into the light, the long, blessed light of the eternity of the people of God, into the everlasting light of the Saviour's presence, the soul of little Elsie had passed' (231). The death of random strangers is commonly written into otherwise work-a-day tales of Christmas. Charlotte Maria Haven's *Christmas Hours* (Boston, 1858) represents an extended family gathering at a country house for the holiday season. Their deeply religious discourse circles around Jesus and death, with the girls in the family visiting a local seventeen-year-old, Alice, just 'as the shadows of death gathered over the young girl's countenance, she moved not nor spoke. It was a new and holy scene, – this triumph of faith over sorrow, suffering, and death!' (92). This 'triumph' is represented as a sort of Christmas present in itself. O. F. Walton's *Angel's Christmas* (London, *c.*1880) also represents the death of a very minor character, which convinces Angel's mother, *roman-à-clef* style, finally to accept Jesus, because '*Death* won't take that excuse [i.e. that there is lots of time later for preparation] when *he* knocks on the door' (39). Walton's text is a depressing one, staged in a locus of 'drunken husband, a mangle, and five children!' (5), but there is little to prepare a buyer or reader that the content is so dismal. The hard binding is a festive red, embossed with flowers and a full-colour painting of a bouquet, making this expensive gift book something of a hidden terror. Only the publisher, the Religious Tract Society, might signal more serious topics to a prospective purchaser.

Most children's Christmas books, when they represent death at all, do not make it ancillary to the narrative: the protagonist or a close family member in these cases is killed off. John Strange Winter, Frances E. Crompton, and Mrs Molesworth's *A Christmas Fairy and Other Stories* (Philadelphia, PA, 1900) includes Crompton's 'In the Chimney Corner', which depicts a stillbirth from the perspective of very young children, four and six years old: 'God had sent us a baby sister on that dreadful evening. But then He saw that He could take better care of her than even Mother and Nurse, and He loved her so much that He sent an angel to fetch her away again' (47). Mary J. Holmes' *Christmas Font, a Story for Young Folks* (New York, 1868) concerns a Sunday school that loses Berkie, a little boy who attends. Another boy comments, 'I cannot wish him back, though his

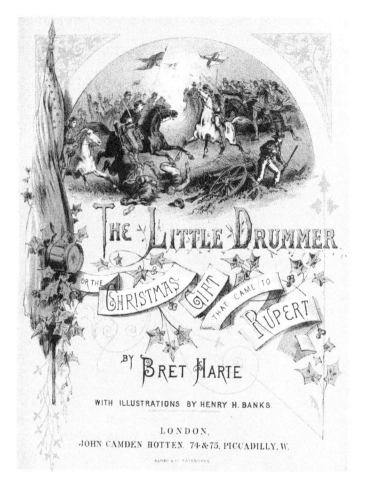

Figure 17 Brett Harte, *The Little Drummer* (London, *c*.1873), title page – Baldwin Library, University of Florida – 39h1165

going from us made a sad vacancy in our little school, and left his parents' hearts so desolate' (18). The death happens, unusually, early in the narrative, and festivities are soon restored, including a tableau of Santa Claus at the school. Unlike the death books published by religious societies, this one has a jolly ending.

Some books trace the entire life of a child protagonist through a Christmas narrative. Bret Harte's *The Little Drummer, or The Christmas Gift That Came to Rupert* (London, c.1873) concerns a Californian boy who receives a toy drum for Christmas. He becomes a young army drummer, and in his dying breath reports: 'The work is done, and I am content. Tell father, it is better as it is. I should have lived only to worry and perplex him, and something in me tells me this is right' (56).

Mrs Molesworth's *A Christmas Child: A Sketch of a Boy-Life* (London, 1880) depicts, over 200 pages, the minor adventures of baby Ted, born on Boxing Day. In the end:

> Ted did not live to see Christmas or his birthday. Sweetly and peacefully, trusting God in death as he had trusted Him in life, the little fellow fearlessly entered the dark valley. . . .
>
> So, children, I will not say that this was the *end* of the simple life I have told you of – and in yet another way Ted lives – in the hearts of all that loved him his sweet memory can never die. (222)

Molesworth's narrative, illustrated by Walter Crane, celebrates even so brief a life and somehow manages to avoid the sentimentality of other Christmas death stories. As a contrasting example, Kate Douglas Wiggin's *The Birds' Christmas Carol* (Boston and New York, 1892) has Carol, 'a very happy baby', born on Christmas day, and then mysteriously die (64). Wiggin includes Alice Ercle Hunt's illustration of Carol dead in her bed (66), not hiding the gravity of the book's contents. Although death is so prevalent in children's Christmas books in the 1850–1910 period, it is very rarely mentioned in the titles and paratexts of these books, and even more rarely illustrated. Publishers rightly seem shy to advertise the mortal contents of books primarily meant for the gift market.

It is little surprise that Christmas books for children from 1850 to 1910 should often take an adultist approach to their intended readership. Christian publishers in particular are keen to tap into a ready market that might reform the impious, especially given the season. Such moralising could take many forms, and I have limited the foregoing discussion to dominant strands. The relative novelty of Santa and Christmas trees, introduced in living memory for the earlier part of the period at least, makes them fertile grounds for considerations of nostalgia and the very purpose of the holiday. By and large, however, the movement from Christmas as a religious or communal holiday towards a child-centric one is made complete over this period. And this movement leads to a very different, more celebratory reading experience to the ones explored in this section.

3 The Festive Christmas, 1850–1910

The Christmas book market at the end of the nineteenth century is not solely driven by morality and adultism. A sense that children should experience respite from their daily schooling, and also that family time should be an occasion for fun, begins to develop in holiday stories. This section considers some of the more festive, less didactic children's Christmas books from the latter half of the nineteenth century and the first decade of the twentieth. Recognising that a 'moral' can be found in even the most nonsensical books, I nonetheless separate out the types of works published by Sunday school leagues and the like from these more commercial ventures.

The Saturday Review, a London literary periodical, offers suggestive addresses to the changing fashions of Christmas books in its annual considerations of them across much of this period. In 1868 it argues stridently for de-moralising Christmas stories: 'Now and then a horrid suspicion crosses us that the boys have been over lectured, over good-booked, and over Tom-Browned and sermonized' ('Christmas Books', 28 November 1868, 729). The same journal's review of Aunt Louisa's books from two years earlier eviscerates seasonal sanctimoniousness:

> One or two of these affairs represent a class which we view with the greatest aversion – the Bible narratives brought down, as it is thought, to infant comprehension. *The Story of King David* is an example; the 'moral' of the history of Bathsheba being, 'Do you not think that David must have been very much ashamed?'
>
> 'Christmas Books', 15 December 1866, 743

Many works of this period make their anti-didacticism apparent from the beginning to avoid just such charges of simplistic moralising. *The Christmas Box: A Christmas and New Year's Present for the Young* (New York, 1865), despite the use of an old-fashioned, pre-stocking term, 'box', tries to appear modern, with a work that purports in the preface to be 'a relaxation from the graver studies of youth' (5). Instead:

> The stories and verses which compose the present volume are designed expressly for the delight of young people. The fairy legends are partly from an American and partly from an European source; and a portion of the poetical effusions are entirely original. (5)

The exact same prefatory statement is given in *Santa Claus, His Friend St. Nicholas, and Kriss Kringle. A Christmas Story Book* (New York, 1876). Being 'entirely original' in this context must be taken with a grain of salt. As with the moral tales discussed in Section 2, even seemingly cheerful titles might reproduce stories, moral or otherwise, that had already been published and that might have little to do with the season. As *The Saturday Review* put it in 1864: 'We must observe that the terms Gift Book and Christmas Book are construed by bookmakers and booksellers with considerable and perplexing laxity' ('Christmas Books', 17 December 1864,

759). Therefore the organisational framework here often requires an examination of titles, prefatory materials, and other paratexts to determine what is meant to appeal to a buyer who might never become familiar with the actual contents.

Doubtless gift copies come to dominate the market. As Simon Eliot's detailed figures have shown, 'the size and importance of the Christmas season (October–December) grew dramatically in the period from 1850 to 1890' ('Some Trends in British Book Production, 1800–1919', 1995, 34); by the 1860s, one-third of all book sales took place in the weeks before Christmas. As Christmas sales begin to drive the entire children's book market, publishers become increasingly willing to invest in striking covers and expensive illustrations – formatting designed to attract the eye of a busy buyer. The growing Christmas market seems at times to have led to a diminution in the quality of written content for children, but to an increase in and an increasing emphasis on the quality of illustration, book production, and design – the elements that might immediately appeal to a buyer. *The Saturday Review* wryly comments of early Christmas books: 'We used to think, the *raison d'etre* of a Christmas book should be its prettiness and flimsiness and unsubstantiality' ('Christmas Books', *The Saturday Review*, 15 December 1866, 743). But by mid-century such books are characterised by 'the fine binding, the gold and scarlet, purple and badger skins' ('Christmas Books', *The Saturday Review*, 21 December 1867, 791),[14] and Christmas books are on 'the principle of the booksellers ... anything in a fine cover' ('Christmas Books', *The Saturday Review*, 15 December 1866, 743). For the most part, this practice makes for pretty but boring literature:

> The field which has produced so luxuriant a crop of Christmas-books seems to have been nearly worked out. The publishers content themselves, for the most part, with issuing our old familiar friends ... the Christmas drawing-

---

[14] 'Badger skins' is a wry reference to the King James Version of the Bible, which has them cover the Ark of the Covenant, and therefore Moses' Tablets of Law (Numbers 4:6). The point is that publishers of children's books present them overindulgently, not that real badger skins are used for binding.

room table presents few innovations. ... Hashed mutton
may put in its claim to acceptance if the Christmas bill of fare
announces it as *Salmi de Noel* [*sic*]. (2 December 1865, 711)

By and large this section slices through quite a bit of salami, but it is
noteworthy that this period also sees the books of Lewis Carroll,
Walter Crane, Randolph Caldecott, Kate Greenaway, and other great
children's authors and illustrators published for the Christmas market,
although not necessarily with Christmas content. A willing cadre of
seasonal publishers, booksellers, and buyers permits such brilliance to
grow and thrive.

Catching the Eye

Over the course of the nineteenth century, Christmas books for children
grow more aesthetically pleasing. Especially prominent is the use of gilt
edging or gold tooling in bindings. This section explores these techniques
for attracting the adult buyer and the child reader, and how the 'throwaway'
genre of Christmas annuals and 'gift books' becomes supplemented by
limited-edition books to treasure.

Especially popular are bright covers with gilt accents, in colours now
strongly associated with the holidays. Santa's suit becomes its customary
red in this period, after representations for children in yellow, green, and
brown, and red is also seen as an attractive colour for children's books.
Lewis Carroll insists on red for his *Alice's Adventures in Wonderland* as
'*bright red* will be the best ... the most attractive [colour] to childish
eyes' (Cohen and Gandolfo, *Lewis Carroll*, 1987, 35). *Holiday Stories with
Many Pictures* (New York, 1850), at the beginning of this period,
provides an embossed red cover with gilt-edged paper. *The Christmas
Box* (New York, 1865), published at the same time as *Alice's Adventures
in Wonderland*, like that book uses red cloth and gilt lettering, as does, at
the end of the century, Thomas Nelson Page's *Santa Claus's Partner*
(New York, 1899). Green and gold are also popular for the more
expensive end of the market, as in Caldecott's illustrated version of
Irving's *Old Christmas* (1876; Figure 18).

Figure 18 Washington Irving, *Old Christmas*, illust. Randolph Caldecott
(London, 1876), cover – Baldwin Library, University of Florida – 23h19542

Multicolour printed covers also grow increasingly common. Sophie May's *Lill's Travels* (London, 1878) combines a bright red binding with a four-colour scene on the cover. *Christmas Joys* (Chicago, 1899) depicts children looking enviously into a toy-shop window on its cover (Figure 19), deploying shades of red and blue and an almost garish amount of gold.

The development and perfecting of chromolithography in the nineteenth century made it possible to produce full-colour images, including on covers, affordably. Laurie Loring's *Snow Flakes from Santa's Land* (New York, 1882) is a lavishly illustrated book, effectively a picturebook, in that each page of prose or verse is augmented with a facing illustration, with a bright cover of a paradoxically unsnowy scene (Figure 20). *Jolly Santa Claus Stories* (New York, c.1901), on the other hand, is a relatively cheap cloth-bound book, with an opportunistic gathering of stories. Yet it too is able to take advantage of cheaper colour printing techniques to attract potential buyers (Figure 21). *Original Christmas Stories* (New York, 1873) reveals just how far colour permeates even the lower end of the market (Figure 22). The book in fact is freely given as a 'Holiday Gift to the Patrons of the Boys' Department / From Baldwin the Clothier'. The rear cover represents Santa carrying a suit of boy's clothing, presumably after shopping at Baldwin. Such an ephemeral book is lucky to survive, a testament in part to the production values given even to promotional materials such as Christmas gift books.[15]

The latter half of the nineteenth century sees much greater variety in size, form, and cost for the gift market. As gift books grow more lavish, they also grow – literally. The *Santa Claus Story Book* (New York, 1875) runs to more than 600 pages. The mishmash of stories is non-consecutively paginated and has a variety of fonts and illustrations, pointing to an assemblage made whole with little more than the binding and title page. The volume has nothing to do with the holidays, but with so much content, it might well provide a year's worth of reading. Vandegrift's *Holidays at Home*, while

---

[15] A more famous example, but outside of the time frame of this Element, is *Rudolph the Red-Nosed Reindeer*, written for the Montgomery Ward department store and distributed free to customers in 1939 (Restad, *Christmas in America*, 1995, 164–6).

Figure 19 *Christmas Joys* (Chicago, 1899), cover – Baldwin Library, University of Florida – 39h117

Figure 20 Laurie Loring, *Snow Flakes from Santa's Land* (New York, 1882), cover – Baldwin Library, University of Florida – 23h11971

only just over 300 pages, is a hefty folio that would challenge the strength of any child. At the other end of the scale, novel formats could be tiny.

Figure 21 *Jolly Santa Claus Stories* (New York, *c.*1901), cover – Baldwin Library, University of Florida – 39h4967

Figure 22 *Original Christmas Stories* (New York, 1873), cover – Baldwin
Library, University of Florida – 23p609

Livingston's *A Visit from St Nicholas* is published by L. Prang (1864) as an accordion miniature book (5 cm by 9 cm when folded), with a yellow-suited Santa and almost unreadably small text. Dorr's *Santa Claus Souvenir* (New York, 1882) loops yarn on the front and rear covers to simulate Santa's beard and hair (Figure 23). It also includes raised details on the front and rear covers and printing in full colour, with Santa once again in golden-yellow furs. As Neil Armstrong notes, 'there was a rich variety of visual representations of Santa Claus in the nineteenth century, and the iconography remained unstable until the twentieth century' ('England and German Christmas', 2008, 489).

Such difficult-to-produce books show how far the market had come from the standard 10 cm by 15 cm paper pamphlets of earlier in the century. Cheap books still appear, of course, and indeed gaudy books might be cheaply produced.[16] Susan Warner's *The Christmas Stocking* (London, *c.*1900), for instance, is priced at 'ONE PENNY' on the cover (Figure 24). It is a paper-bound slip of a book, much shortening the story of *Carl Krinken* that had appeared in 1854.

In general, the new formats of expensive Christmas books that so vexed the annual writers in *The Saturday Review* supplement this cheaper end of the market. That the expensive books survive disproportionately in the archives is perhaps no surprise, given that a one-penny book is effectively disposable reading material. The lavish books, however, are, as Carroll put things, 'most attractive to childish eyes' (Cohen and Gandolfo, *Lewis Carroll*, 1987, 35) – or at least adult authors, publishers, and buyers seem to have seen them in this light.

Addressing the Young Reader

As well as attracting the eyes of young readers, Christmas books of this period also take child interests more seriously through content. Although the trend for bundling various stories under a Christmas wrapping continued, the lore of Christmas becomes deeper and more likely to feature in new books for the season. Prefaces begin to appeal directly to the child reader. T. Stork's

[16] 'It was a curious case of pretence on the one hand and cheapness on the other' for books in this period (Goldman, *Victorian Illustrated Books*, 1994, 72).

Figure 23 Julia C. R. Dorr, *Santa Claus Souvenir* (New York, 1882), cover –
Baldwin Library, University of Florida – 39p644

*A Christmas Book for Children: Containing Luther's Christmas Tree and Jesus in
the Temple* (Philadelphia, PA, *c.*1858) steers young readers' expectations in
looking for 'joy': 'Dear Children: – This little book has been prepared for you
as a Christmas gift. May it help to remind you of the Christ-child, whose

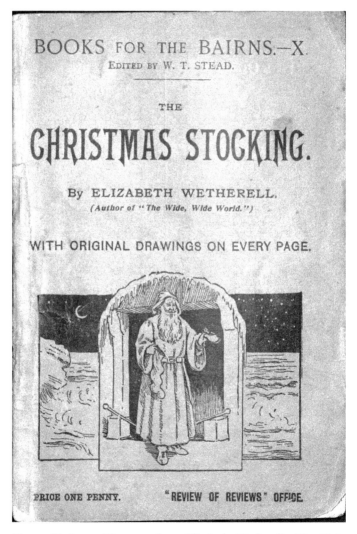

Figure 24 Susan Warner, adapt. Elizabeth Wetherell, *The Christmas Stocking* (London, *c*.1900), cover – Baldwin Library, University of Florida – 23p2165

returning birth-day lights up your homes with mutual love and innocent joy' (v). Later in the book, childlike concerns over the holidays are followed up too: 'It would be well for us to keep up the German custom of preparing a Christmas Tree. It helps to make Christmas day the special holiday of childhood' (31). Christmas, even in a religious text such as this one, is explicitly for the young. Some prefaces target even younger audiences. Robert St John Corbet's *Mince-Pie Island* (London, *c.*1870s) gives extensive space to the practice of reading his book aloud to children:

> Though throughout the stories in this book I usually address myself to little readers, I have designed them rather for little listeners, knowing well that juvenile folk derive far more pleasure from listening than from reading. ... A mamma, aunt, or that invaluable piece of adorableness, a grown-up sister, can make interest in a story almost a certainty for little listeners, by looks of astonishment, by exclamations, and judicious pauses at certain points. (np)

Christmas reading here is an act for female grown-ups, taking us a long way from the 'mansplained' Christmas morals of earlier in the century.

While the metatexts of Christmas books for children take the child reader (or listener) more seriously, the stories too adopt a child-centric approach. An unadulterated focus on the joys of presents emerges, without the moral condemnation or emphasis on charity that I discuss in Section 2. A. M. Diaz's *Merry Christmas: Little Stories for Little Folks* (Boston, 1880) shows how such texts exalt in the pleasure of waiting to open one's presents:

> The stockings were hung over her fireplace last evening. What will there be in them? Picture books? blocks? marbles? thimbles? dolls? balls? tops? clothes? new shoes? ribbons? ruffles? reins? rattles? jumping jacks? sugar dogs? sugar horses? sugar elephants? (np)

In Mary Seymour's *Mollie's Christmas Stocking* (Boston, 1869), one child hopes for 'a new doll, with eyes that will open and shut' (7) – a surprisingly frequent request. The most famous representation of joy over Christmas presents is E. T. A. Hoffman's *Nutcracker and Mouse-King*, which is translated by Mrs St Simon for publication by Appleton in 1853. Although the nut-cracker is the central present of the story, it is worth recalling the inundation of gifts received, uncritically, by Maria and Fred: 'the prettiest dolls, a tea set, all kinds of nice little furniture, and what eclipsed all the rest, a silk dress tastefully ornamented . . . before her eyes, so that she could view it on every side . . . new bay horse [i.e. hobbyhorse] . . . new regiment of hussars' (12). Somewhat wryly, it is only after the children have examined all of their toys that they turn to the gift books also waiting for them:

> The children had now become somewhat more composed, and turned to the picture books, which lay open on the table, where all kinds of beautiful flowers, and gayly dressed people, and boys and girls at play, were painted as natural as if they were alive. (13)

In addition to toys, authors appeal to younger children also by developing the long tradition of animal stories. Lucy Ellen Guernsey's *Tabby's Travels; or, The Holiday Adventures of a Kitten* (New York, 1858) details the lucky escapes of a runaway cat across 200 pages. Often the more pot-luck collections of stories, like Vandegrift's *Holidays at Home*, have a disproportionate number of animal ones when targeting a younger audience. Vandegrift's 'Mince and Stew', for instance, tells of a kitten learning to keep its paws to itself after being pinched by a crab. Distinct from the moralising tradition, then, a less sanctimonious version of the holiday emerges, with direct addresses to children and child-centred stories. This movement aligns with the holiday itself becoming more focused on the child experience, and especially with the rise of Santa Claus.

The Dominance of Santa

From mid-century Santa Claus becomes such a dominant figure of the US holidays – almost as prevalent as gift-giving itself – that it would be impossible to recount all of the various children's books that mythologise him. As some of the bright and lavish covers discussed earlier indicate, Santa Claus is an essential component in garnering American child interest in Christmas books, although he is less prominent until the very end of this period in Britain. What is perhaps unexpected, given the canonisation of Livingston's *A Visit from St Nicholas*, is the willingness of authors to *re*-mythologise him. Santa becomes a fully fleshed character over this period, with a wife, elves, and a host of animal helpers. Because of his ubiquity, this section of this Element is one of the longest, aiming to trace the changing face, duties, and placement of Santa across his formative adolescence.

Section 2 examined the mild backlash the period attempted, mainly on religious grounds, against Santa Claus. That is, of course, a losing battle.[17] By this period children's Christmas books could even poke fun at religious attempts to disparage Santa. *Plays for Little Folks: Santa Claus at Home* (Boston, 1883) is a wry attempt to integrate him into a Christian tradition.

> He is an Orthodox,† – behold him, – he is an Orthodox† . . .
> For he himself has said it,
> And 't is greatly to his credit
> That he is an Orthodox.†
> For he might have been a Quaker,
> A Papist, or a Shaker,
> Or, perhaps, a Unitarian (or an *Orthodox*).
> But in spite of all temptations
> To belong to denominations,
> He remains an Orthodox.† (17)

A little note gives sense to the dagger: '† A Methodist, Universalist, Unitarian, a Baptist true' (17), indicating that the saint could be comfortably fit into most denominations – pointedly excluding Catholics, Quakers, and

---

[17] For an example of continued backlash, see Janet Gill and Theodora Papatheodorou: 'Adults who usually engage in open and rational communications with children appear to be willing to deceive them' ('Perpetuating the Father Christmas Story', 1999, 195).

Figure 25 Sophie May, *Lill's Travels in Santa Claus Land* (Boston, 1878), np – Baldwin Library, University of Florida – 23h1036

Shakers. The book advertises itself as a 'Play for Sunday Schools', actually used by 'First Church Sunday School of Quincy' Massachusetts (4). The Baldwin Library copy includes extensive annotation towards performance by a grammar school. Santa could also be deployed to show overly zealous characters the error of their conservative ways. George C. Lorimer's *Under the Evergreens; or, A Night with St. Nicholas* (Boston, 1875) represents the story of 'Hezekiah Jonah . . . a Puritan in religion' (8), whose 'special horror was the increasing observance among Protestant Christians of the Christmas season . . . To him, it was the evidence of declension in piety, and of a willingness to submit to the authority of Romanism' (9–10). Here, intriguingly opposed to the 1883 play, it is supposedly 'papists' who act as advocates for Santa. Over 180 pages, Santa Claus magically shows up and takes Hezekiah for a sleigh ride, teaching him 'a kinder policy' in the end (180). When Janet Gill and Theodora Papatheodorou ask 'what kind of spirituality could be possibly revealed in the Father Christmas figure?' ('Perpetuating the Father Christmas Story', 1999, 204), they obviously have not considered Victorian versions. Santa, in fact, can show as a participant in a startling variety of religious activity in this period.

Sometimes children do not quite succeed in getting to meet Father Christmas, of course, no matter how hard they try. Laurie Loring's senti-mental *Snow Flakes from Santa's Land* (New York, 1882), for instance, is a mixed collection of stories that includes some harsh content dealing with illness and death, but in the story 'Looking for Santa Claus', a very young child sets out to find him, gets very cold, and 'then he has to go home without seeing Santa Claus. But dear, kind mamma kisses away his tears, and warms and comforts him' (28). For the most part, however, Santa is not only very much present in books for children, but he is extraordinarily varied. In the aforementioned *Original Christmas Stories* for boys who shop at Baldwin the Clothier (1873), fairy tale characters from throughout the canon come to Santa's aid on Christmas Eve. He receives the assistance of Goody-Two-Shoes, Jack the Killer of Giants, Old Mother Hubbard, and Jack Horner (28). Sophie May's *Lill's Travels* stages another example of Santa's home. Here toys are grown in 'a large garden' with 'dolls and donkeys and drays and cars and croquet coming up in long, straight rows' (1878, np). Significantly, the idea that Santa has been around forever is also expressed in May's book – it makes sense that, as a supernatural entity, he could not have been invented by adults in that very century. So Santa says, 'I've been the same age ever since the chroniclers began to take notes,' not pointing out that such notetaking begins with the generation of Lill's grandparents (np). Lill also gets to meet the reindeer, so important from Livingston's poem, but sometimes forgotten in the revised mythologies immediately thereafter.

The trope of children actually meeting Santa appears frequently in this period. In Amanda M. Douglas' *Santa Claus Land* (Boston, 1874) he explains why he is typically so shy: 'I should never get around if the children staid up. They would bother me to death with questions, and want to see their gifts right away, and there would be no end of a fuss' (17). Douglas' Santa also justifies how he is able to cover so much ground: 'O, I have stables and stables full of reindeer, and when I am in a hurry I send out several of the men' (44). It takes a while for the team of reindeer to stabilise to eight, before Rudolf at least, and to receive consistent names. In Mary J. Holmes' *The Christmas Font, a Story for Young Folks* (New York, 1868), a tableau of Santa Claus is made for children, which

> elicited peals of laughter as he drove in his eight reindeer, each with pasteboard horns tied on his head, and his name pinned on his back in large capitals. There were DASHER and DANCER, and PRANCER and VIXEN. There were COMET and CUPID, and DUNDER and BLITZEN; and the little bells about their necks made a soft, tinkling sound, as they shook their horned heads, and pranced in imitation of deer. (50)

Frequently the deer are not named, pointing to a willingness to escape the hagiography of Livingston's *A Visit from St Nicholas*, but even that poem has the names shift slightly in republications. Thomas Nelson Page writes two books in this period that represent children visiting Santa. In the rather benign *Santa Claus's Partner* (New York, 1899) Page recasts the Scrooge story so that an old, redeemed miser takes a young girl named Kitty to choose presents for local poor children. Kitty deeply impresses Santa, who leaves her a letter:

> It stated that the night before, as the writer was engaged in looking after presents for some poor children, he saw a little girl in a shop engaged in the same work, and when he reached a certain hospital he found that she had been there, too, before him, and now as he had to go to another part of the world to keep ahead of the sun, he hoped that she would still act for him and look after his business here.
>
> The letter was signed,
>
> Your partner, Santa Claus (162–3)

Figure 26 *Christmas Boxes* (New York, 1880), np – Baldwin Library, University of Florida – 39p250

In Page's more challenging *Tommy Trot's Visit to Santa Claus* (New York, 1908), two boys go to the North Pole expressly to hunt polar bears. After learning about Santa's generosity and preference for boys who eschew presents but give them out instead, the boys manage to shoot a bear, 'aiming straight between the two eyes' (86). Santa here advocates a kind of muscular but kind manliness, stepping beyond the bounds of his normal charitable role.

An especially elaborate reimagining of Father Christmas comes in
L. Frank Baum's *The Life and Adventures of Santa Claus*
(Indianapolis, IN, 1902). Crucially, by the beginning of the twentieth
century a sense of Santa's timelessness becomes firmly entrenched, so
Baum is able to situate him as the founder of Christmas festive
practice. Santa becomes the originator of not just the Christmas
gift, but of all toys, which did not exist 'until Santa Claus began
his travels' (153). Baum then explains that fireside stockings come
about because of children drying them after building a snowman,
which Santa thinks is a good idea:

> The children's stockings were so long that it required a great
> many toys to fill them, and soon Claus found there were other
> things besides toys that children love. So he sent some of the
> Fairies, who were always his good friends, into the Tropics,
> from whence they returned with great bags full of oranges
> and bananas which they had plucked from the trees. (166)

His idea for a Christmas tree comes because of, it seems dismayingly hinted,
the supposed ignorance of indigenous peoples:

> A Fairy came to Claus and told him of three little children
> who lived beneath a rude tent of skins on a broad plain
> where there were no trees whatever. These poor babies were
> miserable and unhappy, for their parents were ignorant
> people who neglected them sadly. Claus resolved to visit
> these children before he returned home, and during his ride
> he picked up the bushy top of a pine tree which the wind had
> broken off and placed it in his sledge. (167)

Baum is especially creative, and he suffers from characteristic cultural
imperialism, which we will unfortunately see again in twenty-first-
century accounts of Santa. His biography of Santa is nonetheless one
of the most detailed in this period, and sets the stage for the idea that
Christmas is orchestrated in all of its elements from the North Pole.

Santa Claus does not achieve this dominance alone. Although elves are rare (mentioned only by Douglas 1874 in my pre-1910 reading), Mrs Claus receives a life of her own, in America at least. Mrs Claus appears to permit some domesticity to the otherwise (as in Page 1908) heartily masculine Santa. An early mention of Santa's wife comes in Grace Murray's *Happy Christmas* (New York, c.1860), which has a frontispiece illustration of Mrs Claus festooned with toys tied to her waist and arms. The premise is that 'Mrs Claus' wants to come for a holiday visit at the same time as Aunt Kitty. After Aunt Kitty visits, dressed as Mrs Claus, the children 'had a great laugh over our guess that Aunt Kitty and Mrs. Santa Claus were one and the same person. Such a capital Mrs. Santa Claus she was too!' (46). This feminisation of the dressing-as-Santa tradition is fairly unusual in the period. Representations of the 'real' Mrs Claus – not a dressed-up adult – are common. *Christmas Boxes* (New York, 1880) is a large-format picturebook with a peculiar narrative framework. The story begins with Harry Reckless, a young boy, beating a small dog to death. Santa, who sees all good and bad behaviour, wants to strip Harry of his annual presents, but Mrs Claus intervenes:

> Then up, and spoke the buxom dame;
> A kind, and feeling heart had she!
> 'Dear husband, though your judgment blame,
> With mercy, let it tempered be;
> We'll try his heart, with grief and pain,
> But lead him back to hope again'. (np)

Harry indeed learns remorse and receives a lavish Christmas box, equal to that of his brother, Frank Best, in the end.

Mrs Claus can also be represented as rather sterner than her husband in this period. Douglas' *Santa Claus Land* (1874) gives a very full physical and attitudinal description:

> An old woman came hobbling in, leaning heavily on a stick. She was not quite so fat or so jolly as Santa Claus, for you see she had to go round scolding the servants, and looking after everything, while he sat in the chimney-corner

smoking his pipe, and it had taken the flesh off of her bones. Then she had lost some of her teeth, and was bent in the shoulders. She wore a cap with a wide, crimped ruffle, as white as snow. There was a large bow on the top, to make her look taller, I suppose. Then she wore a short-gown, all trimmed with gold braid and velvet leaves, and a scarlet skirt short enough to show her white clocked stockings, and her small ankles, of which she was very proud. She had a wide golden girdle at her waist, from which depended a very gorgeous silken pocket, holding her snuff-box and hand-kerchief. (30)

Doubtless Douglas' prose reveals more about contemporary gender and age stereotypes than the festive season, but it also hints at the idea of a 'lazy' Santa. Emily Hare in *Little Blossom's Reward* (Boston, 1860) had suggested such lethargy by having a Santa who proclaims, 'I'll undertake the thankless office no more; they may go to the toy shops and buy their own toys' (35). Eventually he delivers gifts on New Year's Day, recalling the shift from New Year's as the locus of gift-giving. The circa 1897 book *Santa Claus, Kriss Kringle or St. Nicholas* (Providence, RI) illustrates Mrs Claus as a giant compared to Santa, harking back to earlier representations of him as diminutive:

> My wife, she often calls me hub,
> And, strange to you, sometimes just bub,
> No doubt you think me six feet, four,
> And that I weigh a ton or more,
> But when at home I'm rather small,
> Not near so large nor half so tall
> As when I visit girls and boys
> And load them down with pretty toys. (np)

Santa explains his ability to change size, which becomes crucial to his down-the-chimney mythos once actual adults start to dress up as him. A curious feminised Santa comes in Annie Fellows Johnston's *Miss Santa Claus of the*

Pullman, published in New York in 1913. The story revolves around children who journey by train to meet a new stepmother. A young woman in the carriage, called Miss Santa Claus by a passing boy, because she is in fur, assures them that their new mother might be very nice, as indeed she proves.

Alongside actual representations of Santa and Mrs Claus are books that use 'Santa' in the title – the Baldwin Library holds forty-six from 1850 to 1910, including *Mother Santa Claus Stories* and *Dr Santa Claus Cure*. (Interestingly, the library has only two books with 'Father Christmas' in the title across this period, showing how slow the mingling of Santa Claus and Father Christmas is for children's books.) These works often make very little direct reference to Santa or even to Christmas. Miss Planché's *Santa Claus Annual: A Christmas and New Year's Gift* (New York, *c*.1876), for instance, is an opportunistic gathering of stories published elsewhere that have nothing to do with Christmas. *Father Christmas' ABC* (London, 1894), on the other hand, cleverly comes up with twenty-six festive items, including 'Zany, a clown at a Pantomime' and the ever-popular 'Apples, that Auntie will bring' (np), and shows how Father Christmas and Santa effectively merge in Britain just before the turn of the century. Given that the Baldwin Library holds 404 books with 'Christmas' in the title across this period, Santa books come up to around 10 per cent of that market by title (with an even larger share by content). He becomes a convenient way for publishers and editors to signal jollity – an escape from the heavy-handed moralising bemoaned by *The Saturday Review*. In short, Santa is shorthand for the promise of toys itself, as in Clifton Bingham's picturebook, *Christmas Morning* (New York, 1890):

> It was true! Santa Claus had been – wasn't he kind? –
> He'd left toys and presents for each one behind. (np)

No doubt Santa also helped adult buyers looking for a relaxing Christmas, as he is a powerful secularising force. Just like the protagonist in the anonymous picturebook *Around the World with Santa-Claus* (New York, *c*.1891), at the end of a long holiday evening, sometimes it is nice to relax with a large glass of claret.

The late nineteenth and early twentieth centuries, then, are split by two competing senses of the purpose of Christmas. A residual culture, particularly in the United States, works to remind children that Christmas is about the birth of Christianity itself, while for the United Kingdom the moral Christmas is about charitable giving to those suffering misfortune in the community. An emergent, secularised culture relies upon stockings, gifts, trees, and Santa to make the season one of, paradoxically, old-fashioned 'holiday' – a space of revelry and letting off steam. These rival strands lead to some theologically and culturally complex Christmas books, to be sure, making the period rich in its variety of stories, book formats, and markets. Most of these elements survive in varying guises into the twentieth century.

4 Christmas Books for Children in the Twenty-First Century

Over the 250-year history of children's Christmas books, publishers have learned a great deal from early attempts to establish a viable genre. This section considers how publishing trends from 1800 to 1910 become transformed in contemporary Christmas books. Late in 2018, Amazon.co.uk listed more than 30,000 titles under the search headings of 'Christmas' and 'Children's Books'. These showcase an extraordinary variety and of course include older works by Dickens and Dr Seuss. Equally, any popular character from children's literature, film, or television, including Mickey Mouse, Peter Rabbit, Peppa Pig, Paddington Bear, and Winnie-the-Pooh, also needs a Christmas book. Despite these new faces, Christmas itself has remained a relatively static celebration (Restad, *Christmas in America*, 1995, 155ff.), and most general publishing trends from the nineteenth century survive today, while Christmas sales remain strong, accounting for 20 per cent of the children's book market (Crandall, 'UK Children's Book Business', 2006, 6). One significant change over the twentieth century is the disappearance of luxury Christmas books after World War II (Feather, *History of British Publishing*, 2006, 195). Gold-tooled bindings, or even leather ones, are uncommon, replaced by paperbacks with exceptionally high production quality, but costing little. As such they offer great value, and indeed 'children's books have generally been priced to reflect the means of the putative purchaser, whether it is the child spending pocket money or a cash-strapped parent or teacher purchasing on their behalf' (Crandall, 'UK Children's Book Business', 2006, 3). Despite this shift downmarket – and there were always cheap paperbacks from the very beginning of the genre – children's Christmas books are a static component in gift-giving. Unlike fads associated with toys, books have always been appropriate gifts. And children's Christmases are no more innocent today than they ever were. When Megyn Kelly can gleefully broadcast to millions of her Fox News viewers that 'for all you kids watching at home, Santa just is white' (11 December 2013), it is especially important to consider how Christmas narratives are negotiated today, having the potential to bridge cultural divides as much as to foment them.

This section begins by briefly discussing the familiar elements of Christmas, such as charity, nostalgia, and Santa Claus, that receive a modern twist today. Then it moves to new genres, such as those concerning Hanukkah and Kwanzaa, and the emergence of a teen market. Inevitably, given the explosion of Christmas books today, which includes self-publishing, the works discussed here are a small selection of the market. This section does not attempt to cover the same ground as that of Sections 1–3. Christmas books for children today can pick up and regurgitate any of the tropes that appear in earlier periods. I aim here to select interesting texts that push the boundaries of the Christmas market beyond those established in earlier centuries. I also aim, contra Megyn Kelly, to give space for non-white, non-elite voices – to reflect a fuller diversity than found in the earliest children's Christmas books.

Charity and Migration

Although the long-standing tradition of children reading *A Christmas Carol* has not diminished, and perhaps *because* it has not diminished, the heavy emphasis on charity that one finds in the nineteenth century does not continue as prominently into the twenty-first. Now it is fully accepted that the season, at least from a child's perspective, is about giving and receiving gifts within the family, and less about wider considerations of a needy community. Many of the reinterpretations of the converted-Scrooge theme do not depart significantly from Dickens, almost as if *A Christmas Carol* has frozen that theme. An exception comes in Michael Rosen's *Bah! Humbug!* (London, 2017), which calls itself on the front cover '*A magical retelling of Charles Dickens's* A Christmas Carol'. Here the humbug is the father of the protagonist, Harry. Harry's father continually ignores him in a quest for business success. In a play staged at Harry's school, with the protagonist playing Scrooge, the true Christmas message is revealed, that Christmas is 'the only time ... in the long calendar of the year, when men and women seem to open their shut-up hearts and to think of people below them as if they really were fellow-passengers to the grave' (19). Somewhat sardonically, Rosen makes the point that we need to look after each other, within and without our families.

As the human migration crisis marks the beginning of the twenty-first century, a new strand of charity to non-family and indeed to non-citizens develops in children's books, explicitly countering anti-immigration rhetoric. Anne Booth and Sam Usher's *Refuge* (London, 2015) subtly draws a link between Mary and Joseph's search for sanctuary on the first Christmas and their modern-day counterparts in a beautiful picturebook that represents the new parents as 'hoping for the kindness of strangers' (np). Tanya and Richard Simon's *Oskar and the Eight Blessings* (New York, 2015) explores the position of a German refugee arriving in New York in 1938. Oskar, shipped to America by his parents to flee Nazi persecution, experiences a series of kindnesses from strangers in a touching reminder that the reception of refugees is part of being American.

Latin American migration is a common theme in US Christmas picturebooks. Francisco Jiménez's *The Christmas Gift: El regalo de Navidad* (Boston, 2000), an English and Spanish dual-language book, tells the story of Panchito and his family, who work as migrant farm labourers. Illustrations, by Claire B. Cotts, depict the family's poverty though patched clothing and a leaking roof. The family must follow the crops on below-subsistence wages, 'looking for food in the trash behind grocery stores' (np) and attending school in fleeting spurts. In the end the children receive a small amount of candy at Christmas and are moved to tears. It is an important reminder that the ample material comforts of the holiday in the West are propped up by the hard work of those in extreme need. Harriet Ziefert's *Home for Navidad* (Boston, 2003) depicts the pain caused when a migrant family must live apart. Ten-year-old Rosa stays in Mexico, while her mother has been away as a cleaner in New York for three years. Of course, all Rosa really wants for Christmas is to see her mother again, and in the end she receives her wish, but not without exposing the poverty and hardship experienced by both her and her mother as they work to achieve better lives. Carolyn Marsden's *Mama Had to Work on Christmas* (New York, 2003) tells the story of Gloria, forced to work in a hotel with her mother on Christmas day, and then to cross the border to her grandmother's shabby house for Christmas evening. Gloria, at first horrified by conditions in Mexico, realises how hard her family has fought for a better life. Latinx Christmas books for children are a vibrant part of the market, depicting an incredibly hard-working ethos that recalls *Christmas Greens* (c.1865).

Adultism and Nostalgia Reimagined

Although charity might now seem a little heavy as a Christmas theme for children, adultism and nostalgia are as popular as ever. There is a long-standing wise-head-young-shoulders trope that makes children like Meg in Madeleine L'Engle's *A Wrinkle in Time* (New York, 1962) receive 'a type-writer for Christmas' (50). Beyond that are attempts at adult humour that range from the wry to the condemnatory. A famous example from the twentieth century, remaining popular today, is Raymond Brigg's *Father Christmas* (London and New York, 1973). Briggs is better known for *The Snowman*, reappearing as it does in its 1982 television adaptation every year. *Father Christmas*, however, is not quite so gentle in content, though it won the Kate Greenaway medal in 1973. Santa here is genuinely grumpy at the prospect of delivering gifts: 'Blooming Christmas here again!' (np). After a difficult night of deliveries, he enjoys ale, Christmas pudding, a cigar, and brandy, and is especially pleased with a bottle of cognac he receives as a gift from 'Good Old Fred' (np). Making Santa into a Scrooge reluctant to perform his duties is something we saw in the work of Emily Hare (1860) and Amanda Douglas (1874). Briggs adds a hint of heavy drinking and surly bachelordom to that tradition.

Nostalgic accounts of Christmases past prove to be popular ways for adults to communicate idealised experiences to children. Such nostalgia can be manufactured while being at the same time a key component of negotiating authenticity: 'In the popular imagination Christmas is often perceived to rest upon a series of contradictions, which are predicated on the notion that Christmas past was somehow more "authentic" than Christmas present' (Armstrong, 'England and German Christmas', 2008, 487). Christmas books in the twentieth century often use old holiday pastimes to oppose simplicity to commercialism. Alice Dalgliesh's collection *Christmas: A Book of Stories Old and New* (New York, 1934) notes of Laura Ingalls Wilder's *The Little House in the Big Woods*: 'It is particularly pleasant on these days of a commercialized and elaborate Christmas to read about a Christmas as simple as this one' (230). Susan Cooper's fantasy *The Dark Is Rising* returns to British folk Christmases with wassailing and the yule log. Fantasy Christmas as a kind of pseudo-medieval experience is also part of the Harry Potter series, with the famous festive scene in *Harry Potter and the Chamber of Secrets* (London, 1998) depending upon revelry in the hall and an abundance of food, 'holly and mistletoe' in scenes that recall Irving's *Old Christmas* (162). Owing to its English Civil War setting, Frances Hardinge's *A Skinful of Shadows* (2017) also brings the nostalgic Christmas to young readers, with a boar's head (106), Yule log (107), and local villagers who receive 'plates of tongue, bowls of pale and lumpy brawn, and platters of cheese and apples' (108). One of the most popular Christmas books of 2017 is Jacqueline Wilson's *Hetty Feather's Christmas*. Hetty is Wilson's 'humble foundling' (3) who recalls Christmas in 1888. The old-fashioned holidays include blind man's bluff (134–7) and quite a lot of parody of the old Christmas trope of supporting orphans.

Christmas scenes, as with Rowling and Hardinge, sneak into a variety of children's fantasy texts that sell well in the seasonal market, but are not marketed themselves as Christmas books. A more direct representation of nostalgia comes in Natalie Kinsey-Warnock's *A Christmas Like Helen's* (Boston, 2004). Kinsey-Warnock's picturebook represents what Christmas was like in Vermont around 100 years ago. It is a space of hard work 'all year long' and potential death; when ill 'the doctor didn't expect you to live' (np). It is typical of a strain of Americana that takes pride in the resilience of forebears. But in truth there is not much need for new nostalgic Christmas books as so many old ones already serve that purpose. Families ritualise the rereading such books, from *A Christmas Carol* to *The Snowman*, to each new generation of children.

Santa

Santa Claus is both a figure of tradition and in need of continual update. The scope for that update is fairly limited, however, as in the twentieth century 'advertising helped codify his appearance, particularly Haddon Sundblom's illustrations for Coca-Cola' (Armstrong, 'England and German Christmas', 2008, 489). It would be a very radical Santa indeed to appear in any colour but red, for instance; even Briggs has him wear a bright shade of crimson in an otherwise muted palette. Yet sometimes Santa must face the age of computers or houses without fireplaces.

Tom Fletcher's *Christmasaurus* (London, 2016) appears on the 'Children's and YA Fiction' UK bestseller list at number four for 15 December 2017, making it the top Christmas-related book with sales of more than 16,000 ('Charts Children's', 2017, 26). His 'Musical Edition' added another 9,000 in sales. Fletcher's narrative centres around a toy dinosaur that comes to life for a bullied little boy, but in terms of Christmas traditions, it only slightly extends the characteristic representation of Father Christmas. Santa is 'not just fat, but fat-tastic!' (37). Nonetheless, his extraordinary fitness allows him to enter and exit countless houses quickly: 'He was the fastest runner in the northern hemisphere. He could dance on the tips of his toes like a ballerina. He could backflip and somersault like a giant, stealthy ninja' (37). Matt Haig's *A Boy Called Christmas* (Edinburgh, 2015) engages with the origins of Father Christmas, creating a very human character. Haig gives Nikolas a story of extreme poverty, where his only toy is a doll carved out of a turnip. When his cruel aunt cooks turnip soup, Nikolas decides to run in search for his father in Elfhelm. While there, over a great deal of time, he turns into Father Christmas with the help of the elves, remembering his impoverished past so that other children do not have to suffer without gifts. Haig also wryly points to the difficulty of what to call him, highlighting a common

British misunderstanding about 'Americanisation' of Santa Claus: 'Maybe you don't call him Father Christmas. Maybe you call him something else. . . . It was the pixies who started calling him Santa Claus, and spread the word, just to confuse things, in their mischievous way' (3). Adults do not usually think that 'Father Christmas' should be bringing their children bowls of ale, but the idea that Christmas is 'ours' and not 'theirs' is pervasive. As Judith Flanders writes: 'To most people in Britain, in America, in Germany, Christmas is really a British, American, German holiday' (*Christmas*, 2017, 3). Fletcher and Haig's books are very much for a UK market, with British visions of a Father Christmas (who of course is paradoxically derived from the American Santa Claus, and not the much older English tradition).

A considerably more American approach to elves and Santa working together comes in Carol V. Aebersold and Chanda A. Bell's *Elf on the Shelf: A Christmas Tradition* (Atlanta, GA, 2005). The book is sold with a doll, and just as John Newbery's famous *Pretty Little Pocket Book* came with toys to reward good behaviour in 1744, the little elf is there to surveil, to 'watch and report', on the child (np). Each day the elf is found in a different place, to be discovered in the mornings approaching Christmas. A strong taboo is placed against children actually playing with the elf, perhaps because of his fragile construction: 'The magic might go, and Santa won't hear all I've seen or I know' (np). Arguably, *The Elf on the Shelf* is the most successful children's Christmas book of the twenty-first century, with more than 11 million copies sold, and with several ancillary products, like a birthday edition, just as early nineteenth-century gift series were keen to embrace any cause for celebration. It shows how children's literature has continued to be as much marketing campaign as text (see Nel, 'Is There a Text in This Advertising Campaign?', 2005).

Rod Campbell's *Dear Santa* (London, 2004) is the top-selling UK Christmas-related book for children in the week of 15 December 2017 ('Charts Children's', 2017, 26), highlighting a gap between initial publication and continued sales that itself points to the conservatism of the children's Christmas market. Campbell embraces the 'American' term 'Santa' instead of 'Father Christmas' in this interactive flap book, with presents 'from Santa' on every recto for a child reader to open. Another top seller in 2017 in the United Kingdom is Ian Whybrow and Axel Scheffler's *The Christmas Bear: A Lift-the-Flap Book*, first published in 1998. In it a teddy bear chases after Santa's sleigh to make its way into Tom's pile of presents, as the final flap reveals. These traditional representations of Santa are in keeping with a sense of nostalgic stasis, where festive activities are reinforced through simple narratives of supplying traditional gifts. That these top the bestseller list shows how adult buyers expect children's books to uphold convention. Janet and Allan Ahlberg's *The Jolly Christmas Postman* (London, 1991) also makes the 2017 bestseller list. With its clever reinterpretation of Christmas annuals of old, including games, rebuses, and puzzles, it again appeals to a traditional crossover between book and time-occupying activities for the holiday season.

Terry Pratchett amusingly updates the aging figure in *Father Christmas's Fake Beard*, a 2017 collection of older short stories. Father Christmas does not fit entirely well with a modern, electronics-driven consumer society. He is discovered 'looking at the Meakill Death Cannon (£17.99) . . . and he was very offensive and went on about goodwill to all men' (8). Pratchett even has a dig at Santa's paradoxical foreignness and sameness when trying to get a job in a department store: 'He says he is from the north of Lapland, but I assure him we are an Equal Opportunities Employer, and besides I'm not sure how one would go about discriminating against someone from Lapland, even if one wanted to' (2–3). Santa has to dish out the 'free' gifts for customers who meet him there: 'One plastic Super Laser Zappercon in the case of young males OR one My Little Maddened Polecat Dressing Table Set in the case of young females' (5). Christmas for Pratchett has become violent and gaudy, a far remove from the ideas of 'goodwill' meant to be instilled through Father Christmas. Another modernising take on Santa and elves, one without the irony, comes in Rosie Greening and Clare Fennell's *The Christmas Selfie Contest* (Berkhamsted, 2017). Santa sets up a selfie contest that Alfie the elf attempts to win, before finally deciding that a group 'elfie' is the best approach so that all elves can share in the prize, a sleigh ride. Elves are also emphasised, perhaps in response to *The Elf on the Shelf*, in Mike Brownlow's *Ten Little Elves* (London, 2016), in which Santa's helpers must save Christmas by fetching cough drops for the ill reindeer.

Beyond judging selfies, Santa can find himself in tricky situations in modern children's Christmas books. Rubin Pingk's picturebook *Samurai Santa: A Very Ninja Christmas* (New York, 2015) has him fighting Yukio, a young ninja who thinks that Santa is preventing him and the other ninjas from having fun, as they do not want to appear 'on Santa's NAUGHTY list' (np). When Santa creeps in to deliver presents, he is attacked as an 'INTRUDER' (np) by the ninjas. Santa responds with an army of snowmen, and eventually peace is restored.

Michael Morpurgo's *Grandpa Christmas* (London, 2018) has Mia receive a lengthy letter from her distant grandpa instead of a present or card. The letter recalls a summer of working together in the garden to frame a lengthy discussion about taking care of the planet, arguing against waste and hoping that 'we do not overheat the planet' (np). The comforting illustrations of Grandpa and Mia on the cover and in the beginning of the book do little to prepare buyer or reader for the overt ecological message. It is difficult not to imagine climate-change-denying patriarchs being disappointed with this Christmas present. In the final image Grandpa is dressed as Santa complete with a sack full of toys. Santa here becomes an ecowarrior, as well he should be with the melting polar ice caps.

An attempt to modernise Santa that seems to predict Megyn Kelly's white backlash is Garen Eileen Thomas' *Santa's Kwanzaa* (New York, 2004). The picturebook's cover shows a close-up of Santa's belt, with mittened hands on either side. Santa's skin is carefully hidden in the initial illustrations of the book too. It is only after all of the presents have been delivered that Santa comes home to a black Mrs Claus and black elves, and we see that 'Santa Kwaz' himself is black, with magnificent white dreadlocks. The book then advocates the celebration of Kwanzaa on 26 December. Xavier Garza in *Charro Claus and the Tejas Kid* (El Paso, TX, 2008) has Santa enlist the help of Pancho to deliver toys to children on the US–Mexico border, complete with Flying Burritos that enable them to overcome any concrete walls or wire fences.

Although there are novel appropriations of Santa and his elves in modern children's picturebooks, in the main these offer simple reinterpretations of Santa faithfully delivering his promised toys. Authors and publishers have found varying ways to turn this raw material into bestselling works, taking special advantage of his elves much as the late Victorian canon deployed the novelty of Mrs Claus.

Hanukkah and Kwanzaa

As should be apparent from at least the nineteenth century, the holiday season in children's books has not merely reflected the beliefs of devout Christians – not that such beliefs are unified in any case. Authors and publishers have, long before Donald Trump proclaimed it safe to 'say Merry Christmas again', been able to negotiate these cultural conditions sensitively. Marc Brown's *Arthur's Perfect Christmas* (Boston, 2000), is part of the long-standing Arthur series. Francine, Muffy, and the Brain celebrate Hanukkah, Christmas, and Kwanzaa respectively, and although initially there is a falling out about the importance of these traditions, they come together to respect others' beliefs. These important movements in the Christmas market help a children's publishing industry repeatedly charged with eschewing diversity in favour of profit, and show that overt negotiations of cultural conflict can enable diversification.

A number of books explore the experience of children who have parents with different beliefs. Selina Alko's *Daddy Christmas and Hanukkah Mama* (New York, 2012) is a large picturebook for very early readers, explaining in simple terms ways that Christmas and Hanukkah are celebrated: 'Our tree is crowned with one shiny star. And we light eight candles for Hanukkah' (np). Ilene Cooper's *Sam I Am* (New York, 2004) is a middle-grade version of the mixed tradition, with Sam's father being Jewish and Sam's mother being a secular Christian. Christmas is largely incidental to the story's interest in friendship and school dances, but things become heated when the grandparents come for the holidays: 'The two grandmothers glared at each other' on Christmas Eve because one wants kugel and the other wants mince pie (66). Clay Bonnyman Evans' *The Winter Witch* (New York, 2005) represents the arrival of a new stepmother, Deborah, who places a 'branched menorah over the fireplace, near the Christmas tree' (np) and, worse still to the protagonist, Stephen, 'cooked a salmon that day – a *fish*! For Christmas!' (np). Stephen learns from an old woman in the woods to enjoy all kinds of holiday traditions, and in the end wishes everyone a 'Happy Hanukkah!' too (np). Lemony Snicket takes the perspective of members of the Jewish community tired of overdone Christmas celebrations in *The Latke Who Couldn't Stop Screaming: A Christmas Story* (San Francisco, 2007). The Christmas decorations attempt to normalise the Latke throughout the story, but they just do not get the idea that religions might be different: '"So you're basically hash browns," said the flashing colored lights. "Maybe you can be served alongside a Christmas ham"' (19). The Latke keeps screaming in frustration with the misunderstanding Christmas fanatics around him.

Robert Sabuda, who has published several books about Christmas, has also prepared magical pop-up books to celebrate both Hanukkah and Kwanzaa. Michael J. Rosen and Robert Sabuda's *Chanukah Lights* (Somerville, MA, 2011) is a large, complicated pop-up book with a cover price of 'US $34.99', so perhaps not often given to the younger readers within the vaunted 'ages 5 and up'. The book represents the lighting of each menorah candle in a different location, making a joyful account of the success and happiness of Jewish people around the world today. The back cover notes that the lights 'reflect freedom's promise, hope rekindled amid oppression'. Sabuda's pop-up work for Nancy Williams' *A Kwanzaa Celebration Pop-Up Book* (New York, 1995) is significantly less elaborate than *Chanukah Lights*, and therefore more likely to engage real children. The book carefully explains the origins of Kwanzaa and how each day is celebrated, with a guide to pronunciation: 'Kwanzaa means first fruits of the harvest. On the first day we celebrate Umoja (oo-MOH-jah) or *Unity*' (np). Stressed throughout the book is independence from the Christian tradition: 'Our special history gives us confidence to decide what is important to us. We decide who we are and who we will be' (np). There is no attempt, as in *Santa Kwanzaa*, to unite the two. Andrea Davis Pinkney's *Seven Candles of Kwanzaa* (New York, 1993) is a beautiful picturebook with illustrations by Brian Pinkney. A careful and lengthy 'Note to Readers' explains the origin of Kwanzaa in 1966, while using the same seven-day structure of Williams' book, being careful to remind readers that they do not need to miss out on presents, but also that children 'can give Kwanzaa gifts too' (np).

Interestingly Kwanzaa picturebooks as a genre spend a great deal of time explaining how to celebrate, much as early nineteenth-century children's Christmas books worked to show how novelties like trees and Santa should function. Only more recent books, like Donna L. Washington's *Li'l Rabbit's Kwanzaa* (New York, 2010), build these basic structures into more elaborate narratives. In this case Li'l Rabbit gathers foods so that he can celebrate Karamu – the big feast – with his ill Granna.

Hanukkah and Kwanzaa are of course *not Christmas*, yet these celebrations partake in the children's holiday book market in similar ways to the Christian holiday. Many of them work explicitly *against* the ubiquity of Christmas, either through protest or omission. Those books that represent a mixture of holiday traditions, like *Arthur's Perfect Christmas*, invariably seek tolerance and understanding, not the Christian cultural dominance advocated by some right-wing groups today.

Christmas Teen Romance

The twenty-first-century children's book market is saturated with teen romance and survival books like *Twilight* and *Hunger Games*.[18] The rise of such subgenres within the relatively new young adult (YA) genre has percolated to the Christmas market in recent decades, with a slew of self-published books available. I here consider some of the titles coming out of mainstream publishers. *Ex-mas* by Kate Brian (New York, 2008) tells the love trials of Lila Beckwith, a Los Angeles high schooler who has to endure a holiday road trip with her parents. Stephanie Perkins' collection *My True Love Gave to Me: Twelve Holiday Stories* (London, 2014) includes Hanukkah and New Year's contexts, and homoeroticism. Melissa de la Cruz's *Pride and Prejudice and Mistletoe* (New York, 2017) rewrites Jane Austen's classic for the holidays with an empowered New Yorker, Darcy, who falls in love during a holiday trip home. Rachel Cohn and David Levithan's *The Twelve*

---

[18] The dominance of these subgenres is notably subsiding: see Alison Flood, 'Authors voice alarm after sharp drop in sales of YA fiction', *The Guardian*, 27 February 2019, www.theguardian.com/books/2019/feb/27/authors-voice-alarm-after-sharp-drop-in-sales-of-ya-fiction, accessed 22 July 2019.

Days of Dash and Lily (New York, 2016) is a sequel to their *Dash and Lily's Book of Dares*. Christmas is not particularly festive for Lily, who forgets the joys of Christmas in the light of a great deal of teen angst.

It is perhaps telling that YA takes a back seat to children's books, at least in terms of sales, over the holiday period. The sex and romance often found in the genre do not seem especially festive or familial to modern eyes. But the fact that Christmas is so strongly associated with childhood in itself makes the topic a difficult one for YA, where individuation stands up to tradition and separation from family pastimes is crucial to the genre.

Although the children's Christmas book market is heavily dependent upon older titles, there has been plenty of room for innovation in this century. A more inclusive holiday season has been the aim of many authors and publishers. The charitable end of the market has turned focus onto migrants, and global concerns have come to the fore. Books also represent more diverse celebrants, ensuring that those of a wider range of faiths, sexualities, and identities are included. The commercial fears of earlier centuries are certainly present too, with what some might see as cynical marketing attempts, like *Elf on a Shelf*, offset by the ridicule of them whereby 'children want *so much*' (McCaughrean, *Forever X*, 1997, 12). The split families and orphans so common in the nineteenth century survive today, although there is a greater emphasis on stepparents, and visits by grandparents are certainly more normalised as people live longer. Sex has to a certain extent replaced death, as YA Christmas stories begin to appear.[19] One of the biggest changes relates to the price of books. It is astonishing how inexpensive the UK Christmas bestsellers are, even in hardback. David Walliams' *Bad Dad*, for instance, whatever one thinks of the content, is sold at only £5.97, even though it is a beautifully produced, heavily illustrated hardback of more than 400 pages. Only the elaborate designs of Robert Sabuta qualify as remote cousins to the elaborate gift books of the nineteenth century. On a price-for-quality basis, we appear to be in a new

---

[19] The Baldwin Library, searching by keywords, has ninety books on Christmas and death from 1800 to 1899, and only fifteen books on this combination of topics from 1900 to 1999.

golden age of children's Christmas books. It is to be hoped that the content can match the lavish production values, which, ironically enough, was equally of concern in the Victorian era.

Conclusion

Children's books are not only the products of Christmas; they are equally the producers of it. The Christmas book market has brought forth two of the most popular and important works of children's fiction: Livingston's *A Visit from St Nicholas* and Dicken's *A Christmas Carol*. Both works have been formative in shaping the Christmas of today – a celebration centred around families communing together, especially with children. Neither work, nor the cultural conditions it produces, is likely to go out of fashion any time soon. Yet this conservatism – the fact that there is a ready market for the kinds of works about Christmas that might have been read by children eight generations ago – has not prevented publishers and authors from producing an annual flood of new material. Christmas remains the most important season for the sale of new children's books – whether they are directly concerned with the holiday or not. Christmas thus defines children's literature as much as children's books define it.

This book has showcased the range of children's Christmas books across the nineteenth and the twenty-first centuries. It has not aimed to feature the best of these books, or always the most influential, but instead has focused upon examples that show the diversity of Christmas in the English-speaking world. Christmas is not fully globalised, and local customs shape book-buying habits in surprising ways. Amazon's children's bestsellers on 20 November 2017 in the United Kingdom and the United States has only *The Diary of a Wimpy Kid* as a text featuring in the top ten of both, and such divergence continues throughout the Christmas season. Christmas books therefore surprise with their impressive variety and localism – and although the season itself is suffused with nostalgia and repetition, its literature for children certainly is not.

Bibliography

Aebersold, Carol V. and Chanda A. Bell, *The Elf on the Shelf: A Christmas Tradition*. Illust. Coë Steinwart. Atlanta, GA: CCA and B, 2005.

Ahlberg, Janet and Allan Ahlberg. *The Jolly Christmas Postman*. London: Puffin, 1991; ND [2017].

Alcott, Louisa May. *Little Women*. Boston: Roberts Brothers, 1868.

Alden, Raymond MacDonald. *Why the Chimes Rang*, decorated by Mayo Bunker. Indianapolis, IN: Bobbs-Merrill, 1909.

Alko, Selina. *Daddy Christmas and Hanukkah Mama*. New York: Knopf, 2012.

The Annualette: A Christmas and New Year's Gift. Boston: T. H. Carter, 1844.

Armstrong, Neil. 'England and German Christmas Festlichkeit, c. 1800–1914'. *German History* 26 (2008): 486–503.

Around the World with Santa-Claus. Pictures by R. Andrè. New York: McLoughlin Brothers, *c.*1891.

Aunt Fanny's Christmas Stories. New York: Appleton, 1848.

Aunt Louisa's Sunday Picture Book Comprising Joseph and His Brethren, the Story of King David, the Wonders of Providence, the Proverbs of Solomon. London: Frederick Warne, 1867.

Barbauld, Anna Laetitia and John Aikin, *New Christmas Tales, Forming the Second Part of Evenings at Home*. London: Edward Lacey, ND [*c.*1790].

Baum, L. Frank. *The Life and Adventures of Santa Claus*. Illust. Mary Cowles Clark. Indianapolis, IN: Bowen-Merrill, 1902.

Bible. King James Bible Online. www.kingjamesbibleonline.org. Accessed 6 November 2018.

Bingham, Clifton. *Christmas Morning*. New York: Raphael Tuck, ND [1890].

Booth, Anne and Sam Usher. *Refuge*. London: Nosy Crow, 2015.

Boy's Own Annual. A Holiday Companion for All Seasons. London: Darton, 1861.

Braddon, Mary Elizabeth. *The Christmas Hirelings*. Illust. Frederick Henry Townsend. London: Simpkin, Marshall, Hamilton, Kent, 1894.

Brady, James T. *A Christmas Dream*. Illust. Edward S. Hall. New York: Appleton, 1860.

Brian, Kate. *Ex-mas*. New York: Simon and Schuster, 2008.

Briggs, Raymond. *Father Christmas*. London and New York: Hamish Hamilton, 1973.

Brough, Robert B. *A Cracker Bon-Bon for Christmas Parties: Consisting of Christmas Pieces, for Private Representation, and Other Seasonable Matter, in Prose and Verse*. London: David Bogue, 1852.

Brown, Marc. *Arthur's Perfect Christmas*. Boston: Little, Brown, 2000.

Brownlow, Mike. *Ten Little Elves*. Illust. Simon Rickerty. London: Hachette, 2016.

Buckmaster, Jonathan. '"Ten Thousand Million Delights": Charles Dickens and the Childhood Wonder of the Pantomime Clown'. *Dickens and the Imagined Child*. Ed. Peter Merchant and Catherine Waters. London and New York: Routledge, 2015. Pp. 111–30.

Butcher, Edmund. *The New Year's Gift; or, Moral Tales: Designed to Instruct and Improve the Minds of Youth. From the London Edition*. Boston: Leonard C. Bowles, 1819.

Butterworth, Hezekiah. *The Christmas Book*. Boston: Lothrop, 1891.

Campbell, Rod. *Dear Santa*. London: Macmillan, 2004.

Carroll, Lewis. *Alice's Adventures in Wonderland*. Illust. John Tenniel. London: Macmillan, 1865.

Chamerovzow, Louis Alexis. *The Yule Log: For Everybody's Christmas Hearth, Showing Where It Grew, How It Was Cut and Brought Home, and How It Was Burnt*. Illust. George Cruikshank. London: T. C. Newby, 1847.

'Charts Children's'. *The Bookseller*. 15 December 2017, 26.

Child, Lydia Maria. *The Girl's Own Book*. London: Tegg, Hailes, Bowdery, and Kerby; Glasgow: Griffin, 1832.

The Children's Friend. Number III: A New-Year's Present, to the Little Ones from Five to Twelve ... Containing Eight Coloured Engravings. New York: William B. Gilley, 1821.

Christmas ABC. Philadelphia, PA, and New York: Turner and Fisher, 1844.

Christmas Blossoms and New Year's Wreath. Boston: Phillips and Sampson, 1847.

Christmas Bowers Sparkling with the Brightest Gems from the Mines of Literature ... For Boys and Girls and Older Folk. Philadelphia, PA: Royal, 1892.

The Christmas Box: A Christmas and New Year's Present for the Young. New York: Leavitt and Allen, ND [1865].

Christmas Boxes. New York: McLoughlin, ND [1880].

The Christmas Eve. A Tale from the German. Boston: William Crosby and E. P. Peabody, 1843.

Christmas Greens. Philadelphia, PA: American Sunday-School Union, ND [c.1865].

Christmas Holidays, or The Young Visitants; a Tale; in Which Many Pleasant Descriptions of That Festive Season, Both in Town and Country, Are Given for the Benefit of the Rising Generation. London: J. Harris, 1806.

Christmas Hours. 2nd edn. Boston: Ticknor and Fields, 1859.

Christmas Joys. Stories of Santa Claus, Stories of Adventure, Stories of Hunting, Stories of all Kinds for Boys and Girls. Chicago: W. B. Conkey, 1899.

A Christmas Offering, Humbly Presented by the Charity Children, of Christ Church, in Surrey. London: R. Parsley, 1788.

The Christmas Party. London: Groombridge and Sons, ND [*c*.1850].

Christmas Sports and Other Stories. Boston: Brown, Bazin, 1855.

Christmas Stories, Containing John Wildgoose, the Poacher; The Smuggler; and Good-Nature, or, Parish Matters. 4th edn. London: J. G. and F. Rivington, 1835.

A Christmas Time by 'Pansy'. Boston: D. Lothrop; Dover, NH: G. T. Day, 1875.

The Christmas Tree. A Christmas and New-Year's Gift, from the Children of the 'Warren Street Chapel.' January 1st., 1845. Boston: Office of the Christian World, 1845.

A Christmas Tree for Christ's Children. By a Laborer in the Vineyard. New York: General Protestant Episcopal Sunday School Union, and Church Book Society, 1860.

Cohen, M. N. and A. Gandolfo, eds. *Lewis Carroll and the House of Macmillan*. Cambridge: Cambridge University Press, 1987.

Cohn, Rachel and David Levithan. *The Twelve Days of Dash and Lily*. New York: Knopf, 2016.

Mrs Coleman, *The Mother's Present: A Holiday Gift for the Young*. Boston: S. Colman, 1847.

Collyer, Mary [Mary Homebread], *A Christmass-Box for Masters and Misses*. London: Cooper and Boreman, 1746.

Cooper, Ilene. *Sam I Am*. New York: Scholastic, 2004.

Cooper, Susan. *The Dark Is Rising*. London: Chatto and Windus, 1973.

Corbet, Robert St John. *Mince-Pie Island: A Christmas Story for Mince-Pie Eaters*. London: Cassell, Petter, and Galpin, ND [*c*.1870s].

Cousin Mary, *Christmas Holidays at Chestnut Hill*. Boston: Phillips, Sampson and Co, ND [*c*.1853].

Crandall, Nadia. 'The UK Children's Book Business 1995–2004: A Strategic Analysis'. *New Review of Children's Literature and Librarianship* 12:1 (2006): 1–18.

Croker, T. Crofton, ed. *The Christmas Box, an Annual Present for Children*. London: William Harrison Ainsworth, 1828.

de la Cruz, Melissa. *Pride and Prejudice and Mistletoe*. New York: St Martin's, 2017.

Dalgliesh, Alice, ed. *Christmas: A Book of Stories Old and New*. Illust. Hildegard Woodward. New York: Charles Scribner's Sons, 1934.

Davis, Caroline E. K. *A Christmas Story*. Boston: Ira Bradley, [1868].

Davis, Paul. *The Lives and Times of Ebenezer Scrooge*. New Haven, CT: Yale University Press, 1990.

Diaz, A. M. *Merry Christmas: Little Stories for Little Folks*. Boston: Lothrop, 1880.

Dickens, Charles. *A Christmas Carol: A Pop-Up Book*. [Baltimore, MD]: Allan Publishers, 1989.

Dickens, Charles. *A Christmas Carol. In Prose. Being a Ghost Story of Christmas*. Illust. John Leech. London: Chapman and Hall, 1844 [1843].

Dickens, Charles. *A Christmas Carol: Rewritten for Young Readers by Margaret Waters*. Chicago: Brewer, Barse, and Company, 1907.

Dorr, Julia C. R., ed. *Santa Claus Souvenir*. New York: Baker, Pratt and Company, 1882.

Doughty, S. P. *Playing Santa Claus, and Other Christmas Tales*. Boston: Nichols and Noyes, 1865.

Douglas, Amanda M. *Santa Claus Land*. Boston: Shepard and Gill, 1874.

E., H. S. *The Marleigh Christmas Tree, and What Came of It. A Story for School-Girls*. Illust. L. W. London: Society for Promoting Christian Knowledge, ND [*c*.1870s].

Elihu Lewis: or, The Fatal Christmas Day. Boston: Massachusetts Sabbath School Society, 1848.

Eliot, Simon. 'Some Trends in British Book Production, 1800–1919'. In *Literature in the Marketplace: Nineteenth-Century British Publishing and*

Reading Practices. Ed. John O. Jordan and Robert L. Patten. Cambridge: Cambridge University Press, 1995. Pp. 19–43.

L'Engle, Madeleine *A Wrinkle in Time*. New York: First Square Fish, 1962; rpt. 2007.

Evans, Clay Bonnyman. *The Winter Witch*. Illust. Robert Bender. New York: Holiday House, 2005.

Father Christmas ABC. London and New York: F. Warne, 1894.

Feather, John. *A History of British Publishing*. New York: Routledge, 2006.

A Fireside Book, or The Account of a Christmas Spent at Old Court. 2nd edn. London: Smith, Elder, and Company, 1830.

Flanders, Judith. *Christmas: A Biography*. London: Picador, 2017.

Fletcher, Tom. *The Christmasaurus*. Illust. Shane Devries. London: Puffin, 2016.

Garza, Xavier. *Charro Claus and the Tejas Kid*. El Paso, TX: Cinco Puntos, 2008.

Gems Gathered in Haste: A New Year's Gift for Sunday Schools. Boston: John Wilson & Son, 1851.

Gill, Janet and Theodora Papatheodorou. 'Perpetuating the Father Christmas Story: A Justifiable Lie?', *International Journal of Children's Spirituality* 4 (1999): 195–205.

Glaser, Karina Yan. *The Vanderbeekers of 141st Street*. New York: Houghton Mifflin Harcourt, 2017.

Goldman, Paul. *Victorian Illustrated Books 1850–1870*. London: British Museum, 1994.

Greening, Rosie and Clare Fennell. *The Christmas Selfie Contest*. Berkhamsted: Make Believe, 2017.

Grenby, M. O. *The Child Reader, 1700–1840*. Cambridge: Cambridge University Press, 2011.

Gubar, Marah. 'On Not Defining Children's Literature', *PMLA* 126 (2011): 209–16.

Guernsey, Lucy Ellen. *Tabby's Travels; or, The Holiday Adventures of a Kitten. A Christmas and New-Year's Story*. New York: Anson D. F. Randolph, 1858.

Haig, Matt. *A Boy Called Christmas*. Edinburgh: Canongate, 2015.

Hamilton, Virginia. *Bluish*. London: Scholastic, 1999.

Hardinge, Frances. *A Skinful of Shadows*. London: Macmillan, 2017.

Hare, Emily. *Little Blossom's Reward. A Christmas Book for Children*. Boston: S. C. Perkins, 1860.

Harte, Bret. *The Little Drummer, or The Christmas Gift that Came to Rupert*. Illust. Henry H. Banks. London: John Camden Hotten, ND [*c*.1873].

[Haven, Charlotte Maria.] *Christmas Hours*. 2nd edn. Boston: Tricknor and Fields, 1858.

Herrick, Robert. *The Hesperides and Nobel Numbers*. Ed. Alfred Pollard. Rev. ed. Vol. 2. London and New York: Lawrence and Bullen, 1898.

History of the Christmas Festival, the New Year, and Their Peculiar Customs. London: G. Newcomb, 1843.

Hoffman, E. T. A. *Nutcracker and Mouse-King*. Trans. Mrs St Simon. New York: Appleton, 1853.

Holiday Stories with Many Pictures. New York: Samuel Raynor, 1850.

Holmes, Mary J. *The Christmas Font, a Story for Young Folks*. New York: G. W. Carleton; London, S. Low, Son, and Company, 1868.

[Hughs, Mary]. *Aunt Mary's New Year's Gift to Good Little Boys and Girls Who Are Learning to Read*. London: William Darton, 1819.

Immel, Andrea. '*A Christmass-Box*, Mary Homebred and Mary Collyer: Connecting the Dots'. *Children's Books History Society Newsletter* 94 (December 2009): 1–5.

Irving, Washington. *Old Christmas: From the Sketch Book of Washington Irving*. Illust. Randolph Caldecott. London: Macmillan, 1876.

Jackson, MacDonald P. *Who Wrote 'The Night Before Christmas'? Analyzing the Clement Clarke Moore vs. Henry Livingston Question.* Jefferson, NC: McFarland, 2016.

Jaques, Zoe and Eugene Giddens. *Lewis Carroll's* Alice's Adventures in Wonderland *and* Through the Looking-Glass*: A Publishing History.* Farnham: Ashgate, 2013.

Jiménez, Francisco. *The Christmas Gift: El regalo de Navidad.* Illust. Claire B. Cotts. Boston: Houghton Mifflin, 2000.

Jolly Santa Claus Stories. New York: McLoughlin, ND [c.1901].

Johnston, Annie Fellows. *Miss Santa Claus of the Pullman.* Illust. Reginald B. Birch. New York: Century, 1913.

Jonson, Ben. *Christmas His Masque* in *Workes.* London: Thomas Walkley, 1641.

Julia Changed; or, The True Secret of a Happy Christmas. Philadelphia, PA: American Sunday School Union, 1831.

Kilner, Dorothy. *The Holyday Present.* London: J. Marshall, c.1781.

Kinsey-Warnock, Natalie. *A Christmas Like Helen's.* Boston: Houghton Mifflin, 2004.

Kriss Kringle's Christmas Tree: A Holiday Present for Boys and Girls. Philadelphia, PA, 1847.

Lamb, Martha J. *Merry Christmas.* Boston: Gould and Lincoln, 1870.

Lawson, Lizzie and Robert Ellice Mack. *Christmas Roses.* New York: E. P. Dutton, ND [c.1886].

Leslie, Eliza, ed. *The Gift: A Christmas and New Year's Present for 1839.* Philadelphia, PA: E. L. Carey and A. Hart, 1838.

The Literary Box: Containing the Contributions of the Evelyn Family. Philadelphia, PA: Ash and Mason, ND [1826].

[Livingston, Henry] Moore, Clement C. *A Visit from St Nicholas.* With original cuts, designed and engraved by Boyd. New York: Spalding and Shepard, 1849.

[Livingston, Henry] Moore, Clement C. *A Visit from St Nicholas*. Boston: L. Prang, 1864.

[Livingston, Henry]. *Visit of St Nicholas*. Illust. Thomas Nast. Aunt Louisa's Big Picture Series. New York: McLoughlin, ND [c.1872].

[Livingston, Henry.] *A Visit from Santa Claus*. Illust. David Scattergood. Boston : Degen, Estes & Company, ND [c.1880].

Locke, Una and Frances Lee. *Holiday Tales*. Boston: American Tract Society, 1863.

Lorimer, George C. *Under the Evergreens; or, A Night with St. Nicholas*. Boston: Lovering, 1875.

Loring, Laurie. *Snow Flakes from Santa's Land*. New York: Thomas V. Crowell, 1882.

McCaughrean, Geraldine. *Forever X*. Oxford: Oxford University Press, 1997; 2001.

Martineau, Harriet. *Christmas Day; or, The Friends, a Tale*. London: Houlston, 1825.

Martineau, Harriet. *The Friends: A Continuation of 'Christmas-Day'*. London: Wellington, Salop, 1826.

Marsden, Carolyn. *Mama Had to Work on Christmas*. Illust. Robert Casilla. New York: Viking, 2003.

Mathews, Joanna H. *Elsie's Santa Claus*. New York: Robert Carter, 1876.

May, Sophie, et al. *Lill's Travels in Santa Claus Land and Other Stories*. Boston: D. Lothrop, 1878.

Mince Pies for Christmas, and for All Merry Seasons: Consisting of Riddles, Charades Rebuses, Transpositions and Queries: Intended to Gratify the Mental Taste, and to Exercise the Ingenuity of All Sensible Masters and Misses. A New Edition. London: Tabart, 1807.

Mrs Molesworth. *A Christmas Child: A Sketch of a Boy-Life*. Illust. Walter Crane. London: Macmillan, 1880.

Morpurgo, Michael. *Grandpa's Christmas*. Illust. Jim Field. London: Egmont, 2018.

Murray, Grace. *Happy Christmas*. New York: Sunday-School Union, ND [*c*.1860].

Murray, T. B. *Christmas-Tide, and Its Customs*. New York: General Protestant Episcopal Sunday School Union, and Church Book Society, 1860.

Nel, Philip. 'Is There a Text in This Advertising Campaign? Literature, Marketing, and Harry Potter'. *The Lion and the Unicorn* 29 (2005): 236–67.

A New-Year's Gift. New York: S. Wood, 1809.

A New Year's Gift: From the Children of the Warren Street Chapel. Boston, January 1, 1841. Boston: Tuttle and Dennett, 1841.

Nikolajeva, Maria. *Power, Voice and Subjectivity in Literature for Young Readers*. New York: Routledge, 2010.

Nikolajeva, Maria. *Reading for Learning: Cognitive Approaches to Children's Literature*. John Benjamins Publishing Company, 2014.

Nissenbaum, Stephen. *The Battle for Christmas*. New York: Knopf, 1996.

Nurse Truelove's Christmas-Box; or, The Golden Plaything for Little Children. London: John Newbery, *c*.1750.

Nurse Truelove's New-Year's Gift; or, The Book of Books for Children. London: John Newbery, *c*.1750.

O'Brien, Charlotte. *The Cottagers' Christmas*. London: Office of the Family Economist, 1856.

Optic, Oliver. *The Christmas Gift. A Story for Little Folks*. Boston: Lee and Shepard, 1863.

Original Christmas Stories: The Ball of the Fruits, Little Betty, The Naughty Little Squirrel, and How They Helped Santa Claus. New York: Baldwin the Clothier, 1873.

Original Tales; Never before Published. Designed as a New-Year's Gift for the Youth of Both Sexes. Boston: Charles Callender, 1813.

Page, Thomas Nelson. *Santa Claus's Partner*. Illust. W. Glackens. New York: Charles Scribner's Sons, 1899.

Page, Thomas Nelson. *Tommy Trot's Visit to Santa Claus*, illustrated by Victor C. Anderson. New York: Charles Scribner's Sons, 1908.

Parker, Theodore. *The Two Christmas Celebrations, A. D. I and MDCCLV. A Christmas Story for MDCCCLVI*. Boston: Rufus Leighton, 1859.

Parry, J. D. *The Anthology: An Annual Reward Book for Midsummer and Christmas*. London: Whittaker, Treacher and Company, 1830.

Perkins, Stephanie, ed., *My True Love Gave to Me: Twelve Holiday Stories*. London: St Martin's Griffin, 2014.

Pindar, Susan. *Fireside Fairies: or Christmas at Aunt Elsie's*. New York: Appleton, 1850.

Pingk, Rubin. *Samurai Santa: A Very Ninja Christmas*. New York: Simon and Schuster, 2015.

Pinkney, Andrea Davis. *Seven Candles for Kwanzaa*. Illust. Brian Pinkney. New York: Dial, 1993.

Miss Planché [Mrs Henry S. Mackarness]. *The Santa Claus Annual: A Christmas and New Year's Gift*. New York: Leavitt and Allen, ND [*c.*1876].

Plays for Little Folks: Santa Claus at Home. Boston: Walter H. Baker, 1883.

Pratchett, Terry. *Father Christmas's Fake Beard*. Illust. Mark Beech. London: Doubleday, 2017.

A Present for Children: Containing, Dr. I Watt's Second Set of Catechisms . . . 2nd edn. Edinburgh: William Gray, 1761.

Pullman, Philip. *The Book of Dust*. Oxford: David Fickling, 2017.

Rand, Edward A. *Christmas Jack*. New York: American Tract Society, 1878.

Restad, Penne L. *Christmas in America: A History*. New York: Oxford University Press, 1995.

Rosen, Michael. *Bah! Humbug!* Illust. Tony Ross. London: Scholastic, 2017.

Rosen, Michael J. and Robert Sabuda. *Chanukah Lights*. Somerville, MA: Candlewick Press, 2011.

Rowling, J. K. *Harry Potter and the Chamber of Secrets*. Illust. Jim Kay. London: Bloomsbury, 2016; 1998.

Saint Nicholas's Book: For All Good Boys and Girls. Philadelphia, PA: Thomas Cowperthwait, 1842.

Sandham, E. *The Grandfather; or The Christmas Holidays*. London: Bowdery and Kerby, 1816.

Santa Claus, His Friend St. Nicholas, and Kriss Kringle. A Christmas Story Book. Three Volumes in One. New York: World Publishing, 1876.

Santa Claus, Kriss Kringle or St. Nicholas. Providence, RI: E. J. White, ND [c.1897].

Santa Claus Story Book. New York: Leavitt & Allen, 1875.

Sargent, George E. and Myra, et al. *The Holly Tree: A Winter Gift*. Illust. Dickes. London: Benjamin L. Green, 1850.

The Saturday Review of Politics, Literature, Science, and Art. London: 1863–7.

Schlicke, Paul, ed. 'Chapman and Hall'. In *The Oxford Companion to Charles Dickens: Anniversary Edition*. Oxford: Oxford University Press, 1999; 2011. Pp. 71–6.

von Schmid, Christoph. *The Christmas Eve. A Tale from the German*. Boston: William Crosby and E. P. Peabody, 1843.

[Selwyn, A.] *A New Year's Gift; or, Domestic Tales for Children*. London: Hodgson, 1824.

S[eymour], M[ary] H. *Mollie's Christmas Stocking*. Boston: Dutton, 1869.

Shropshire, Elmo and Patsy Trigg. 'Grandma Got Run Over by a Reindeer'. *Grandma Got Run Over by a Reindeer*. Elmo 'n' Patsy, 1978.

Simon, Tanya and Richard Simon. *Oskar and the Eight Blessings*. Illust. Mark Siegel. New York: Roaring Brook, 2015.

Sinnett, Mrs Percy. *A Story about a Christmas in the Seventeenth Century*. London: Chapman and Hall, 1846.

Snicket, Lemony. *The Latke Who Couldn't Stop Screaming: A Christmas Story*. Illust. Lisa Brown. San Francisco: McSweeney's, 2007.

[Sobersides, Solomon]. *Christmas Tales for the Amusement and Instruction of Young Ladies and Gentlemen in Winter Evenings*. Hudson, NY: Ashbel Stoddard, 1794.

[Somerville, Elizabeth.] *A Birth Day Present; or A New Year's Gift. Being Nine Day's Conversation between a Mother and Daughter, on Interesting Subjects; for the Use of Young Persons, from Ten to Fifteen Years of Age*. Boston: David Carlisle, 1803.

Standiford, Les. *The Man Who Invented Christmas: How Charles Dickens's* A Christmas Carol *Rescued His Career and Revived Our Holiday Spirits*. New York: Broadway, 2008; 2017.

Stork, T. *A Christmas Book for Children: Containing Luther's Christmas Tree and Jesus in the Temple*. Philadelphia, PA: Lindsay and Blakiston, ND [c.1858].

Swan, Annie S. *Katie's Christmas Lesson*. New edn. Edinburgh: Oliphant, Anderson, and Ferrier, ND [c.1880].

Thayer, William M. *Merry Christmas, a Christmas Present for Children and Youth*. Boston: Stone and Halpine, 1854.

Thomas, Garen Eileen. *Santa's Kwanzaa*. Illust. Guy Francis. New York: Hyperion, 2004.

Towne, Belle K. and T. Martin Towne. *Santa Claus' Dream, A Christmas Cantata for the Use of Sunday-Schools*. Chicago: David G. Cook, 1894.

Vandegrift, Margaret [Margaret Thomson Janvier], *Holidays at Home: For Boys and Girls*. Philadelphia, PA: Porter and Coates, 1882.

The Violet: A Christmas and New Year's Gift. With six engravings from designs by Gilbert. New York: Leavitt and Allen, ND [1858].

Walliams, David. *Bad Dad*. Illust. Tony Ross. London: Harper Collins, 2017.

Walton, O. F. *Angel's Christmas*. London: Religious Tract Society, ND [*c*.1880].

Waring, Susie M. *Diamonds and Rubies; or The Home of Santa Claus*. New York: W. H. Kelley and Brother, 1864.

Warner, Susan. *Carl Krinken: His Christmas Stocking*. New York: G. P. Putnam, 1854.

Warner, Susan, adapt. Elizabeth Wetherell. *The Christmas Stocking*. 6th edn. London: Review of Reviews Office, ND [*c*.1900].

The Warning Clock, or, The Voice of the New Year. By the Author of 'The Two Lambs,' &c. New York: Mahlon Day, 1829.

Washington, Donna L. *Li'l Rabbit's Kwanzaa*. Illust. Shane W. Evans. New York: Harper Collins, 2010.

Webster, George P. *Santa Claus and His Works*. Aunt Louisa's Big Picture Book series. New York: McLoughlin Brothers, ND [*c*.1872].

Wheatly, Sarah. *The Christmas Fire-Side; or, The Juvenile Critics*. London: Longman, Hurst, Rees, and Orme, 1806.

Whybrow, Ian and Axel Scheffler. *The Christmas Bear: A Lift-the-Flap Book*. London: Macmillan, 1998; reprinted 2016.

Wiggin, Kate Douglas. *The Birds' Christmas Carol*. Boston and New York: Houghton Mifflin, 1892.

Wiggin, Kate Douglas. *The Romance of a Christmas Card*. Illust. Alice Ercle Hunt. Boston and New York: Houghton Mifflin, 1916.

Williams, Nancy. *A Kwanzaa Celebration Pop-Up Book*. Illust. Robert Sabuda. New York: Little Simon, 1995.

Wilson, Jacqueline. *Hetty Feather's Christmas*. Illust. Nick Sharratt. London: Corgi, 2017.

Winter, John Strange, Frances E. Crompton, and Mrs Molesworth. *A Christmas Fairy and Other Stories*. Philadelphia, PA: Henry Altemus, 1900.

Yonge, Charlotte Mary, ed., *Alice's Watch: A Christmas Story*. London: Frederick Warne, *c.*1870s.

Ziefert, Harriet. *Home for Navidad*. Illust. Santiago Cohen. Boston: Houghton Mifflin, 2003.

Acknowledgements

Research towards this Element has benefitted from the kind hospitality of the Baldwin Library of Historical Children's Literature, University of Florida; School of Information and Library Science, University of North Carolina; and the Harry Elkins Widener and Caroline Miller Parker collections at Harvard University. Much of the work conducted in those libraries was towards a longer-term project on children's book illustration in the nineteenth century. I have been lucky to have encountered many Christmas books and gift copies over the course of that research. Thanks goes to the University of Florida for support of this project through a Travel to Special Collections Grant. I am especially grateful to the curator of the Baldwin Collection, Suzan Alteri, and to Michele Wilbanks for assistance with digitisation.

The idea for this Element comes from Zoe Jaques, without whose daily support and critical reading it would not exist. Fox Benwell and Stephen Mortimer have been very helpful readers. Teresa Grant and colleagues in English literature at Anglia Ruskin have been generous with their recommendations of Christmas books.

Cambridge Elements $\equiv$

Publishing and Book Culture

SERIES EDITOR

Samantha Rayner

University College London

Samantha Rayner is a Reader in UCL's Department of
Information Studies. She is also Director of UCL's Centre for
Publishing, co-Director of the Bloomsbury CHAPTER
(Communication History, Authorship, Publishing, Textual
Editing and Reading) and co-editor of the Academic Book of
the Future BOOC (Book as Open Online Content) with UCL
Press.

ASSOCIATE EDITOR

Rebecca Lyons

University of Bristol

Rebecca Lyons is a Teaching Fellow at the University of
Bristol. She is also co-editor of the experimental BOOC (Book
as Open Online Content) at UCL Press. She teaches and
researches book and reading history, particularly female own-
ers and readers of Arthurian literature in fifteenth- and six-
teenth-century England, and also has research interests in
digital academic publishing.

ABOUT THE SERIES

This series aims to fill the demand for easily accessible, quality texts available for teaching and research in the diverse and dynamic fields of Publishing and Book Culture. Rigorously researched and peer-reviewed Elements will be published under themes, or 'Gatherings'. These Elements should be the first check point for researchers or students working on that area of publishing and book trade history and practice: we hope that, situated so logically at Cambridge University Press, where academic publishing in the UK began, it will develop to create an unrivalled space where these histories and practices can be investigated and preserved.

Cambridge Elements ⁼

Publishing and Book Culture
Children's Literature

Gathering Editor: Eugene Giddens

Eugene Giddens is Skinner-Young Professor of Shakespeare and Renaissance Literature at Anglia Ruskin University. His work considers the history of the book from the early modern period to the present. He is co-author of *Lewis Carroll's* Alice's Adventures in Wonderland *and* Through the Looking-Glass: *A Publishing History* (2013).

ELEMENTS IN THE GATHERING

Picture-Book Professors: Academia and Children's Literature
Melissa Terras

Christmas Books for Children
Eugene Giddens

A full series listing is available at: www.cambridge.org/EPBC

CPSIA information can be obtained
at www.ICGtesting.com
Printed in the USA
LVHW082100261119
638464LV00017B/990/P